MW01107663

Arabic

PHRASE BOOK

Compiled by
LEXUS
with
R'kia Iguider Colville
and
Michael Parry

HARRAP

EDINBURGH   PARIS

Distributed in the United States by
PRENTICE HALL
New York

First published in Great Britain 1993
by CHAMBERS HARRAP PUBLISHERS LTD
43-45 Annandale Street, Edinburgh EH7 4AZ, UK

ISBN 0 245 50201 7

In the United States ISBN 0 671 84765 1

Library of Congress Cataloguing-in-Publication Data

Harrap's Arabic phrase book
p.   cm.
English and Arabic.
Includes grammar section and currency conversion tables.
ISBN 0 671 84765 1
I. Arabic language ≈ Conversion and phrase books ≈ English. II. Title.
PJ6309.P63   1993   93-18485
492'.783421 ≈ dc20   CIP

Cover photograph US Edition: Steve Vidler/Leo de Wys Inc.
Printed in England by Clays Ltd, St Ives plc

CONTENTS

Abbreviations used in this book

adj	adjective
f	feminine
m	masculine
pl	plural
prep	preposition
(R)	registered trademark
sing	singular

INTRODUCTION

The phrase sections in this book are concise and to the point. In each section you will find: a list of basic vocabulary; a selection of useful phrases; a list of common words and expressions that you will see on signs and notices. A full pronunciation guide is given for things you'll want to say or ask and typical replies to some of your questions are listed.

Of course, there are bound to be occasions when you want to know more. So this book allows for this by giving an English-Arabic dictionary with a total of some 1,700 references. This will enable you to build up your Arabic vocabulary and to make variations on the phrases in the phrase sections.

As well as this, we have given a menu reader covering about 200 dishes and types of food - so that you will know what you are ordering! And, as a special feature, there is a section on colloquial Arabic.

The section on Things Arabic gives cultural information about Arabic-speaking countries as well as some notes on the language.

Speaking the language can make all the difference to your trip. So:

حظ سعيد !

HaZZ saAeed!
good luck!

and

سفرة طيبة !

safra Tayiba!
have a good trip!

THE ARABIC ALPHABET

	Final	Middle	Initial	Letter in isolation
a	ل	ل	ا / أ	ا / أ
b	ـب	ـبـ	بـ	ب
t	ـت	ـتـ	تـ	ت
th	ـث	ـثـ	ثـ	ث
j/g	ـج	ـجـ	جـ	ج
H	ـح	ـحـ	حـ	ح
kh	ـخ	ـخـ	خـ	خ
d	ـد	ـد	د	د
z	ـذ	ـذ	ذ	ذ
z	ـز	ـز	ز	ز
r	ـر	ـر	ر	ر
s	ـس	ـسـ	سـ	س
sh	ـش	ـشـ	شـ	ش
S	ـص	ـصـ	صـ	ص
D	ـض	ـضـ	ضـ	ض
T	ـط	ـطـ	طـ	ط
Z	ـظ	ـظـ	ظـ	ظ
A	ـع	ـعـ	عـ	ع
gh	ـغ	ـغـ	غـ	غ
f	ـف	ـفـ	فـ	ف
q	ـق	ـقـ	قـ	ق
k	ـك	ـكـ	كـ	ك
l	ـل	ـلـ	لـ	ل
m	ـم	ـمـ	مـ	م
n	ـن	ـنـ	نـ	ن
w	ـو	ـو	و	و
h	ـه	ـهـ	هـ	ه
y	ـي ، ـى	ـيـ	يـ	ي

PRONUNCIATION

In the phrase sections of this book a pronunciation guide has been given by writing the Arabic words as though they were English. So, if you read out the pronunciation as English words, an Arabic-speaker should be able to understand you. Some notes on this:

a   as in 'bad'
aa long 'a' as in 'car'
A   a forced 'a' as in 'had' but with greater emphasis
aw as in 'jaw'
ay as in 'fray'
D   a forced 'd'; try saying 'dabble' with a strong emphasis on the 'd'
e   as in 'bed'
gh similar to a French 'r'
H   a forced 'h'; try saying 'heavy' with a strong emphasis on the 'h'
kh as the 'ch' in the Scottish pronunciation of 'loch'
oo as in 'pool'
ow as in 'cow'
q   'c' as in 'can'
S   a forced 's'; try saying 'sulk' with a strong emphasis on the 's'
T   a forced 't'; try saying 'toll' with a strong emphasis on the 't'
th as in 'three'
u   as the 'oo' in 'rook'
Z   a forced 'z'; try saying 'zoo' with a strong emphasis on the 'z'
'   a throaty sound like a catch in the breath

If a vowel represented by a capital letter in the pronunciation is followed or preceded by another vowel, then both are pronounced. When two consonants occur together, both should be pronounced. Letters in bold type in the pronunciation guide mean that this part of the word should be stressed.

GENERAL PHRASES

hello/hi assalaamu Aalaykum	السلام عليكم
good morning SabaH ul-khayr	صباح الخير
good evening masa' ul-khayr	مساء الخير
good night tiSbaH Aala khayr	تصبح على خير
pleased to meet you tasharraft	تشرفت
goodbye/cheerio maAa as-salaama	مع السلامة
see you ila liqaa'	إلى اللقاء
yes naAam	نعم
no laa	لا
yes please naAam, low samaHt	نعم، لو سمحت
no thank you laa, shukran	لا، شكراً
please min faDlek	من فضلك

GENERAL PHRASES

thank you/thanks
shukran

شكراً

thanks very much
shukran jazeelan

شكراً جزيلا

you're welcome
Aafwan

عفوا

sorry
aasif

آسف

sorry? *(didn't understand)*
eesh qult?

إيش قلت ؟

how are you?
kayf al-Haal?

كيف الحال ؟

very well, thank you
Tayyib, al-Hamdu li-laah

طيب، الحمد لله

and yourself?
(said to a man/woman)
wa inta/inti?

و انت ؟

excuse me *(to get attention)*
low samaHt

لو سمحت

can I ...?
mumkin ...?

ممكن ... ؟

can I have ...?
ureed ...

أريد ...

I'd like to ...
mumkin ...?

ممكن ... ؟

I'd like a ...
ureed ...

أريد ...

9

GENERAL PHRASES

where is ...?
ayn ... ?

أين ... ؟

it's not ...
maa ...

ما ...

is it ...?
hal ...?

هل ... ؟

is there ... here?
feeh ... hina?

فيه ... هنا ؟

could you say that again?
aA-id, min faDlek

أعد، من فضلك

could you speak more slowly?
laa tetkallam bi-surAa, min
faDlek

لا تتكلم بسرعة، من فضلك

I don't understand
maa fahimt

ما فهمت

OK
Tayyib

طيب

come on, let's go!
yal-lah, nirooH!

يا الله، نروح !

what's that in Arabic?
ism haaza bi al-Aarabi?

إسم هذا بالعربي ؟

could you write it down?
mumkin tektub al-kilma?

ممكن تكتب الكلمة ؟

I don't speak Arabic
maa at-kallam Aarabi

ما أتكلم عربي

GENERAL PHRASES

الخروج	al-khurooj	exit
الرجاء عدم ...	ar-rajaa' Aadam ...	please do not ...
الرجال	ar-rijaal	gents
السيدات	as-sayidaat	ladies
دخول	dukhool	way in
إدفع	'idfaA	push
إحترس	'iHtaris	caution
إسحب	'isHab	pull
للمسلمين فقط	li al-muslimeen faqaT	Muslims only
للموظفين فقط	li al-muwazzafeen faqaT	staff only
للنساء	li an-nisaa'	ladies
للرجال	li ar-rijaal	gents
ماء صالح للشرب	maa' SaaliH li ash-shurb	drinking water
مفتوح	maftooH	open
مخرج الطوارىء	makhraj at-Tawaari'	emergency exit
ممنوع	mamnooA	forbidden
ممنوع الدخول	mamnooA ad-dukhool	no entry
ممنوع أخد الصور	mamnooA akhd as-Suwwar	no photography
ممنوع الخروج	mamnooAal-khurooj	no exit
ممنوع التدخين	mamnooA at-tadkeen	no smoking
مصعد	masAad	lift
مشغول	mashghool	engaged
مسجد	masjid	mosque
مرحاض	mirHaad	toilets
مغلق	mughlaq	closed
ساعات العمل	saaAaat al-Aamal	opening hours
شاغر	shaaghir	vacant

11

COMING AND GOING

airport	al-maTaar	المطار
baggage	al-Haqaa'ib	الحقائب
book (in advance)	Hajz	حجز
coach	Haafila	حافلة
docks	ar-raSeefIf	الرصيف
ferry	al-qaarib	القارب
gate (at airport)	al-baab	الباب
harbour	al-menaa	الميناء
plane	Taa'ira	طائرة
sleeper	Aarabat an-nowm	عربة النوم
station	maHaTTa	محطة
taxi	taksee	تاكسي
train	qiTaar	قطار
visa	ta'sheera	تأشيرة

a ticket to ...
tazkira li ...

تنكرة ل ...

I'd like to reserve a seat
ureed aHjiz maqAad

أريد أحجز مقعد

smoking/non-smoking please
makaan mumkin feeh
at-tadkheen/makaan
mamnooA feeh at-tadkheen

مكان ممكن فيه التدخين /
مكان ممنوع فيه التدخين

a window seat please
qurb an-naafiza, min faDlek

قرب النافذة ، من فضلك

which platform is it for ...?
min ayy raSeef ...?

من أي رصيف ... ؟

12

COMING AND GOING

what time is the next flight?
mita ar-riHla al-qaadima?

متى الرحلة القادمة ؟

is this the right train for ...?
haaza huwwa al-qiTaar li ...?

هذا هو القطار ل ... ؟

is this bus going to ...?
al-baaS, yerooH li ...?

الباص ، يروح ل ... ؟

is this seat free?
al-maqAad mashghool?

المقعد مشغول ؟

do I have to change (trains)?
laazim aghayyir (al-qiTaar)?

لازم أغير (القطار) ؟

is this the right stop for ...?
haaza huwwa al-mowqif li ...?

هذا هو الموقف ل ... ؟

is this ticket ok?
haaz at-tazkira SaaliHa?

هذه التذكرة صالحة؟

I want to change my ticket
ureed aghayyir at-tazkira

أريد أغير التذكرة

thanks for a lovely stay
shukran Aalaa Diyaafatkum

شكراً على ضيافتكم

**thanks very much for coming
to meet me**
shukran Aalaa 'stiqbaalak lee

شكراً على استقبالك لي

well, here we are in ...
haa 'iHna waSalna li ...

ها إحنا وصلنا ل ...

إفتح الشنطة ، من فضلك

iftaH eshanTa, min faDlek
**would you mind opening
this bag please?**

13

COMING AND GOING

الحافلات	al-Haafilaat	buses
الخروج	al-khurooj	exit
الخطوط الداخلية	al-khuTooT ad-daakhiliya	domestic
الخطوط الدولية	al-khuTooT ad-dawliya	international
الجمارك	al-jamaarik	customs
الجوازات	al-jawaazaat	passports
المطار	al-maTaar	airport
المسافرين	al-musaafireen	departures
الوصول	al-wuSool	arrivals
التاكسيات	at-taaksiyaat	taxis
حجز التذاكر	Hajz at-tazaakir	reservations
إستعلامات	'istiAlaamaat	information
مخرج الطوارىء	makhraj at-Tawaari'	emergency exit
ممنوع الدخول	mamnooA ad-dukhool	no entry
ممنوع التدخين	mamnooA at-tadkheen	no smoking
ممنوع الوقوف	mamnooA al-wuqoof	no parking
رصيف ...	aSeef ...	platform ...
رحلة رقم ...	riHla ...	flight number ...

GETTING A ROOM

balcony	balkoon	بالكون
bed	sareer	سرير
breakfast	fuToor	فطور
dining room	ghurfat at-TaAam	غرفة الطعام
dinner	Aashaa'	عشاء
double room	ghurfa li-'thnayn	غرفة لإثنين
guesthouse	nazl	نزل
hotel	funduq	فندق
key	miftaaH	مفتاح
lunch	ghadaa'	غداء
night	layla	ليلة
private bathroom	Hammaam khaaS	حمام خاص
reception	al-'istiqbaal	الإستقبال
room	ghurfa	غرفة
shower	doosh	دوش
single room	ghurfa li-shakhS waaHid	غرفة لشخص واحد
with bath	feeha Hammaam	فيها حمام
youth hostel	maskan as-shabeeba	مسكن الشبيبة

do you have a room for one night?

Aindak ghurfa li-layla waaHida?

عندك غرفة لليلة واحدة ؟

do you have a room for one person?

Aindak ghurfa li-shakhS waaHid?

شخص واحد ؟

GETTING A ROOM

do you have a room for two people?
Aindak ghurfa li-'thnayn?

عندك غرفة لإثنين ؟

we'd like to rent a room for a week
nureed eejaar ghurfa li-'usbooA

نريد إيجار غرفة لأسبوع

I'm looking for a good cheap room
ureed ghurfa kwayyisa wa rakheeSa

أريد غرفة كويسة و رخيصة

I have a reservation
Hajazt

حجزت

how much is it?
bikam al-ghurfa?

بكم الغرفة ؟

can I see the room please?
mumkin ashoof al-ghurfa, min faDlek?

ممكن أشوف الغرفة، من فضلك ؟

does that include breakfast?
al-fuToor fi ath-thaman?

الفطور في الثمن ؟

a room overlooking the sea
ghurfa tiTill Aala al-baHr

غرفة تطل على البحر

we'd like to stay another night
nureed nabqa layla ukhra

نريد نبقى ليلة أخرى

we will be arriving late
HaniwSil muta'akhireen

حنوصل متأخرين

can I have my bill please?
al-Hisaab, min faDlek?

الحساب ، من فضلك ؟

GETTING A ROOM

I'll pay cash Ha'adfaA kaash	حادفع كاش
can I pay by credit card? mumkin adfaA bi-biTaaqa?	ممكن أدفع ببطاقة ؟
will you give me a call at 6.30 in the morning? mumkin tiSaHeeni fi as-saaAa sitta wa nuS, bukra as-SubH?	ممكن تصحيني في الساعة ستة و نص، بكرى الصبح ؟
at what time do you serve breakfast/dinner? mita waqt al-fuToor/ al-Aashaa'?	متى وقت الفطور / العشاء ؟
can we have breakfast in our room? mumkin nefTar fi ghurfatna?	ممكن نفطر في غرفتنا ؟
thanks for putting us up shukran Aala Diyaafatkum	شكراً على ضيافتكم

الإستقبال	al'istiqbaal	reception
المطعم	al-maTAam	restaurant
الرجال	ar-rijaal	gents
السيدات	as-sayidaat	ladies
فندق	funduq	hotel
غرف للإيجار	ghuraf li al-'eejaar	rooms to let
مخرج الطوارىء	makhraj at-Tawaari'	emergency exit
مصعد	masAad	lift
نزل	nazl	small hotel

EATING OUT

bill	al-Hisaab	الحساب
coke (R)	kooka	كوكا
dessert	ad-diseer	الدسير
drink (verb)	sharab	شرب
eat	akal	أكل
food	TaAam	طعام
fresh orange	AaSeer burtuqaal	عصير برتقال
lemonade	limonaada	ليمونادة
main course	al-wajba al-'asaasiya	الوجبة الأساسية
menu	qaa'imat at-TaAam	قائمة الطعام
restaurant	maTAam	مطعم
salad	SalaTa	سلطة
service	rasm al-khidma	رسم الخدمة
starter	al-wajba al-'oola	الوجبة الأولى
tip	baqsheesh	بقشيش
waiter	'akh	أخ

a table for three, please
'iHna thalaatha

إحنا ثلاثة

waiter!
yaa 'akh!

يا أخ !

can I see the menu?
mumkin ashoof al-qaa'ima?

ممكن أشوف القائمة ؟

we'd like to order
'iHna mustaAiddeen

إحنا مستعدين

what do you recommend?
eesh tenSaH?

إيش تنصح ؟

EATING OUT

I'd like ... please
Ha 'aakhud ...

حآخذ ...

can I have what he's having?
mumkin 'aakhud nafs
ash-shay'?

ممكن آخذ نفس الشيء ؟

that's for me
haaza lee

هذا لي

some more bread please
mazeed min al-khubz, min
faDlek

مزيد من الخبز ، من فضلك

could we have the bill, please?
al-Hisaab, low samaHt?

الحساب ، لو سمحت ؟

أطباق البيض	aTbaaq al-bayD	egg dishes
أطباق شرقية	aTbaaq sharqiya	oriental dishes
حلويات	Halawiyaat	sweets
خدمة	khidma	service charge
مقهى	maqha	café
مشروبات	mashroobaat	drinks
مشويات	mashwiyaat	grills
مطعم	maTAam	restaurant

ARABIC MENU READER

SALADS

فتوش fattoosh
mixed salad with toasted bread

لوبية بالزيت loobiya bi az-zayt
green bean salad in olive oil

سلاطة بلدي salaaTa baladi
Arab mixed salad of lettuce, tomatoes and cucumber

سلاطة مشوية salaaTa meshwiya
salad of roasted or grilled vegetables

سلاطة بطاطس salaaTat baTaaTes
potato salad

سلاطة فجل salaaTat fejl
radish salad

تبولة tabooleh
tabouleh - cracked wheat salad

DIPS

بيسارة bisaara
Egyptian bean purée

دكة dukkah
dry and crumbly spicy nut dip

فول مدمس fool mudammas
puréed brown Egyptian beans

جبنة بيضة gibneh bayDa
cream cheese dip

حلبة Helba
hot fenugreek dip

حمص بالطحينة Hommus bi at-taHeeneh
hummous - chickpea and sesame dip

متبل mutabbal
aubergine dip

MENU READER

SOUPS

ملوخية	melookhiya **traditional Egyptian soup, made with a spinach-like vegetable**
شربة عدس	shorbat Aadas **lentil soup**
شربة دجاج	shorbat dajaaj **chicken soup**
شربة خضر	shorbat khoDar **vegetable soup**

Other more substantial types of soup are mainly eaten during the month of Ramadan. The most common are:

فتة	fatta **soup with lamb, rice and tomatoes**
حريرة	Hareera **thick soup made with lamb, various pulses and herbs** (Morocco)
شربة الحوت	shorbat al-Hoot **fish soup**

TYPES OF MEAT

بوفتيك	bufteek **steak**
دجاج	dajaaj **chicken**
ديك رومي	deek roomee **turkey**
كلاوي	kalaawee **kidneys**
كبدة	kebda **liver**
لحم عجل	laHm Aajal **veal**
لحم بقر	laHm baqar **beef**
لحم خروف	laHm kharoof **lamb**
لحم مفروم	laHm mafroom **minced meat**

METHODS OF COOKING MEAT OR FISH

بفتيك مقلي bufteek maqli
fried steak

لحم الفرن laHm al-forn
roast meat

لحم مشوي laHm mashwi
grilled meat

سمك مقلي samak maqli
fried fish

سمك مشوي samak mashwi
grilled fish

MEAT AND POULTRY DISHES

بسطيلة basteela
Moroccan pigeon pie *(served on special occasions)*

دجاج محشي dajaaj maHshi
roast chicken stuffed with rice or couscous *(steamed grains of semolina)*

دجاج مقلي dajaaj mqalli
chicken with preserved lemon and olives

فريك fereek
chicken with hard-boiled eggs

حمام بالفريك Hamaam bi al-fereek
pigeon stuffed with green, unripe hulled wheat

كباب لحم kebaab laHm
meat kebab *(usually lamb)*

كشك بالفراخ keshk bi al-firaakh
chicken with yoghurt and onion

كيمة مشوي عماني keema mashwi Aummaani
spicy minced meat

كفتة على شيش kofta Aala sheesh
minced meat kebab

كفتة مبرومة kofta mabrooma
minced meat with nuts

كفتة فراخ koftat firaakh
fried minced chicken balls

MENU READER

كسكس بللحم   kuskus bi al-laHm
couscous (*steamed grains of semolina*)
with a meat stew (*usually lamb*)

لبن أمه   laban ummu
lamb cooked with yoghurt

مقلوبة   maqlooba
meat stewed with aubergines and rice

مشمشية   meshmeshiya
veal with apricots

مشوي   meshwi
**roast leg or shoulder of lamb, or
whole lamb**

طجين برقوق   Tajeen barqooq
lamb stew with prunes

طجين خضر   Tajeen khoDar
lamb stew with vegetables

زيتون مشوي   zaytoon mashwi
meat balls studded with olives

FISH DISHES

حوت مشرمل   Hoot mesharmal
fish baked in spicy marinade

كباب سمك   kebaab samak
fish kebabs

كسكس بالحوت   kuskus bi al-Hoot
couscous (*steamed grains of semolina*)
with fish stew

لفتية بمنتيق   laftiya bi manteeq
squid with turnips

منتيق محمر   manteeq meHammar
fried squid

ناشبوس   naashboos
spicy fried shrimps

أرز بالجمبري   roz bi al-jambari
prawns and rice

سمك بالطحينة   samak bi aTaHeena
fish baked with tahini (*sesame seed
paste*)

سمك محشي بالروز   samak maHshi bi ar-roz
sweet and sour fish stuffed with rice

MENU READER

طاجين بالحوت   Tajeen bi al-Hoot
fish 'tagine' with tomatoes (*cooked slowly in an earthenware pot called a 'tagine'*)

EGG DISHES

عجة بالبصل   Aigga *OR* Aijja bi al-baSal
omelette with onions

عجة بالتوابل   Aigga *OR* Aijja bi at-tawaabil
omelette with herbs

عجة محشية بالبيض   Aigga *OR* Aijja maHshiya bi al-bayD
omelette stuffed with hard-boiled eggs

بيض بكبدة فراخ   bayD bi kibdat firaakh
scrambled eggs with chopped chicken liver

بيض مقلي   bayD maqli
fried eggs

بيض مسلوق   bayD maslooq
boiled eggs

شكشوكة بالخضر   shakshooka bi al-khoDar
sweet pepper and tomato omelette

شكشوكة بالحمة   shakshooka bi al-laHma
scrambled eggs with minced beef

RICE

أرز بالفول   roz bi al-fool
rice with broad beans

أرز بالزعفران   roz bi al-zaAfraan
saffron rice

أرز و شعرية   roz wa shaAriya
rice with vermicelli

STUFFED VEGETABLE DISHES

محشي بصل   maHshi baSal
stuffed onion rolls

محشي فلفل   maHshi felfel
stuffed peppers

محشي كوسة بللبن   maHshi koosa bi al-laban
stuffed courgettes with yoghurt

MENU READER

شيخ محشي طماطم sheikh al-maHshi TamaaTem
stuffed tomatoes
ورق عنب محشي waraq Ainab maHshi
stuffed vine leaves

OTHER VEGETABLE DISHES

عدس بجبة Aadas bi jibba OR gibba
brown lentils
بامية مرسوسة baamia marsoosa
okra in a mould
باذنجان بالجبن baazinjaan bi al-jibn
baked aubergines and cheese
فاصوليا بيضاء faasooliya bayDaa'
white haricot beans
فلافل felaafel
fried chickpea balls
حمص بسبانخ Hommus bi sabaanakh
chickpeas with spinach
كبة kibbeh
**cracked wheat shells with various
stuffings**
سبانخ بالزيت sabaanakh bi az-zayt
spinach in oil
طعمية TaAmiya
deep-fried balls of spicy bean purée
زعلوك zaAlook
**aubergine, tomato and pepper
purée**

STUFFED PASTRIES

These are small pastries with savoury fillings such as
spinach, minced meat, poultry, fish, seafood, herbs and
cream, cheese and nuts. They are known variously
throughout the Arab world as:

بريك brek *(Tunisia)*
بورك / سمبوسك boorak/samboosak *(the Gulf and the
Levant)*
بورك boorek *(Algeria)*

MENU READER

بريوات briw**aa**t *(Morocco)*
سمبوسك samb**oo**sek *(Egypt)*

TYPES OF BREAD

عيش بلدي **Aa**ysh baladi
Arab flat bread *(like pitta bread, but thicker)*

عيش شامي **Aa**ysh sh**aa**mi
round, flat, pitta-type bread

خبز بصلي khubz ba**S**alee
Syrian onion bread

خبز منقش khubz mun**aq**qash
Lebanese spicy bread

لحمة بعجينة la**H**ma bi-**Aa**jeena
Arab pizza

رقائق raqaa'iq
Arabian crispy bread

سلوف بالحلبة sal**oo**f bi al-**H**elba
Yemeni spicy bread

سفينة sfeena
miniature pizzas

سميط sim**ee**T
bread rings coated with sesame seeds

DESSERTS

بقلاوة baql**aa**wa
baclava - very thin, layered pastry and nuts in syrup

بسبوسة basb**oo**sa
semolina cake with syrup

غريبة ghor**ee**ba
almond biscuits

حلويات **H**alawiy**aa**t
dessert

حلوى شباكية **H**alwa shebbakiya
small petal-shaped pastries, deep-fried then laced with honey and sprinkled with sesame seeds

كعب الغزال k**A**b al-ghaz**aa**l
pastries stuffed with ground almond paste

MENU READER

كنافة konaafa
pastry with nuts and syrup
مهلبية muhallabiya
**pudding made from ground rice,
milk and rose water**
قطايف qaTaayif
syrupy pancakes
روز بلبن roz bi-laban
**rice pudding flavoured with rose
water**
سلاطة فواكه salaaTat fawaakeh
fruit salad
أم علي umm Aali
raisin and milk pudding

TRADITIONAL DRINKS

قهوة عربية qahwa Aarabiya
Arab coffee
شای بالنعناع shaay bi an-naAnaaA
mint tea

VEGETABLES

أرنبيط arnabeeT
cauliflower
بامية baamiya
okra
باذنجان baazenjaan
aubergine
بصل baSal
onion
بسلة basillu
peas
بطاطس baTaates
potatoes
فاصوليا faasooliya
green beans
فلفل أخضر felfel akhDar
green pepper
فول fool
broad beans

MENU READER

فجل	fijl	
	white radish	
جرجير	jirjeer	
	watercress	
جزر	juzur	
	carrots	
خرشوف	kharshoof	
	artichokes	
خيار	khiyaar	
	cucumber	
كوسة	koosa	
	courgettes	
كرفس	krafs	
	celery	
كرنب	kuronb	
	cabbage	
لفت	lift	
	turnip	
سبانخ	sabaanekh	
	spinach	
طماطم	TamaaTem	
	tomatoes	
ثوم	thoom *OR* thawm	
	garlic	

FRUIT

عنب	Ainab	
	grapes	
أناناس	ananaas	
	pineapple	
برقوق	barqooq	
	plum	
بطيخ	baTeekh	
	watermelon	
برتقال	burtuqaal	
	orange	
فراولة	farawla	
	strawberries	
خوخ	khookh	
	peach	

MENU READER

مشمش	mishmish	**apricot**
موز	mooz	**banana**
رومان	rommaan	**pomegranate**
شمام	shammaam	**melon**
تين	teen	**figs**
ثمر	thamr	**dates**
تفاح	tufaaH	**apple**

NUTS

عين جمل	Aayn jamal	**walnuts**
بندق	bunduq	**hazelnuts**
فول سوداني	fool sudaanee	**peanuts**
فستق	fustuq	**pistachio nuts**
لوز	lawz OR looz	**almonds**

BASIC FOODS

عسل	Aasal	**honey**
دقيق	daqeeq	**flour**
فلفل أسود	felfel aswad	**black pepper**
حليب	Haleeb	**milk**
جبنة بيضة	jubna bayDa	**salty, white cheese**

MENU READER

جبنة فلاحي jubna fallaaHee
cheese similar to cottage cheese
جبنة رومي jubna roomi
hard cheese
خل khall
vinegar
لبن laban
yoghurt
مربة merabba
jam
ملح milH
salt
سمنة samna
clarified butter
سكر sukkar
sugar
زيت زيتون zayt zaytoon
olive oil
زبدة zubda
butter

HERBS

الريحان ar-rayHaan
basil
بقدونس baqdoones
parsley
حصى البان HaSaa al-baan
rosemary
كزبرة kuzbura
coriander
نعناع naAnaaA
mint
زعتر zaAtar
thyme

SPICES

هيل hayl
cardamom
كمون kammoon
cumin

MENU READER

قرفة qarfa
cinnamon

قرنفل qurunfel
cloves

زعفران zaAfraan
saffron

زنجبيل zanjabeel
ginger

SPICE MIXTURES

هريسة hareesa
fiery Tunisian paste with chillies and garlic

رأس الحنوت ra's al-Hanoot
Moroccan spice mix

طحينة TaHeena
tahini - oily paste made from ground sesame seeds and used to flavour sauces and salads

تقلية taqliya
blend of ground herbs and spices
(thyme, marjoram, roasted sesame seeds, etc)

زعتر zaAtar
blend of ground herbs and spices
(similar to above)

COLLOQUIAL EXPRESSIONS

I'm absolutely knackered
ana mahlook, bi al-marrah
انا مهلوك ، بالمرة

I'm fed up
khalaaS, taAibt
خلاص ، تعبت

you've got to be joking!
timzaH, wa laa shakk!
تمزح ، و لا شك !

it's rubbish (goods etc)
haaza zeft
هذا زفت

get lost!
gheeb Aanni!
غيب عني !

it's a damn nuisance
wa al-laahi, mushkila
و الله ، مشكلة

it's absolutely fantastic!
wa al-laahi, rawAa!
و الله ، روعة !

عبيط	AabeeT	**idiot**
أجنبي	ajnabee	**foreigner**
با لله عليك !	bi al-laah Aalayk!	**for God's sake!**
خواجة	khawaaja	**foreigner** (non-Muslim, Arabian Peninsula)
لعين !	laAeen!	**damn!**
لا قدر الله !	laa qaddara al-laah!	**God forbid!**
ملعون !	malAoon!	**damn!**
نصراني	naSraani	**foreigner** (non-Muslim, North Africa)
أوربي	oorubbee	**Westerner**

GETTING AROUND

bike	darraaja	دراجة
bus	baaS	باص
bus station	maHaTTat al-Haafilaat	محطة الحافلات
car	sayyaara	سيارة
change (trains)	ghayyar	غير
garage (for fuel)	maHaTTat banzeen	محطة بنزين
map	khareeTa	خريطة
motorbike	darraaja naariya	دراجة نارية
petrol	bitrool	بترول
return (ticket)	zahaab wa iyaab	ذهاب و إياب
single	zahaab, faqaT	ذهاب ، فقط
station	maHaTTa	محطة
taxi	taaksee	تاكسي
ticket	tazkira	تذكرة
train	qiTaar	قطار

I'd like to rent a car
ureed asta'jir sayyaara

أريد أستأجر سيارة

how much is it per day?
bikam li al-yowm?

بكم لليوم ؟

when do I have to bring the car back?
mita laazim arajjiA' as-sayaara?

متى لازم أرجع السيارة ؟

I'm heading for ...
ana musaafir li ...

أنا مسافر ل ...

how do I get to ...?
at-Tareeq li ...?

الطريق ل ... ؟

33

GETTING AROUND

REPLIES

على طول	Aala Tool **straight on**
لف يمين / يسار	liff yameen/yasaar **turn right/left**
هو المبنى هناك	huwwa al-mabna hinaak **it's that building there**
هو كان في طريقك	huwwa kaan fi Tareeqek **it's back that way**
الأول / الثاني / الثالث على اليسار	al-'owwal/ath-thaani/ ath-thaalith Aala al-yasaar **first/second/third on the left**

we're just travelling around
nezoor al-manTaqah

نزور المنطقة

I'm a stranger here
ana moo min hina

أنا مو من هنا

is that on the way?
huwwa fi Tareeqi?

هو في طريقي ؟

can I get off here?
mumkin anzel hina?

ممكن أنزل هنا ؟

thanks very much for the lift
shukran Aala al-musaaAada

شكرا على المساعدة

two returns to ... please
ithnayn zahaab wa iyaab li ...

اثنين ذهاب و إياب ل ...

34

what time is the last train back?
mita aakhir qiTaar li ar-rujooA?

متى آخر قطار للرجوع ؟

we want to leave tomorrow and come back the day after
nureed nusaafir bukra wa narjaA baAd bukra

نريد نسافر بكرى و نرجع بعد بكرى

we're coming back the same day
HanirjaA fi nafs al-yowm

حنرجع في نفس اليوم

is this the right platform for ...?
haaza huwwa ar-raSeef li ...?

هذا هو الرصيف ل ... ؟

is this train going to ...?
haaza huwwa al-qiTaar li ...?

هذا هو القطار ل ... ؟

where are we?
iHna fayn?

إحنا فين ؟

which stop is it for ...?
ayy mowqif qareeb min ...?

أي موقف قريب من ... ؟

how far is it to the nearest petrol station?
fayn aqrab maHaTTat banzeen?

فين أقرب محطة بنزين ؟

I need a new tyre
aHtaaj li 'iTaar jadeed

أحتاج لإطار جديد

it's overheating
al-muHarrik saakhin katheer

المحرك ساخن كثير

GETTING AROUND

**there's something wrong with
the brakes**
feeh mushkila fi al-faraamil

فيه مشكلة في الفرامل

عربة بوفيه	Aarabat boofeeh	buffet car
الدرجة الأولى	ad-daraja al-'oolaa	first class
الدرجة الثانية	ad-daraja ath-thaaniya	second class
المعلومات	al-maAloomaat	enquiries, information
المفقودات	al-mafqoodaat	lost property
الطريق السريع	at-Tareeq as-sareeA	motorway
غرفة الإنتظار	ghurfat al-intiZaar	waiting room
احترس	'iHtaris	caution
اتجاه واحد	ittijaah waaHid	one way
خالي	khaali	vacant
خطر	khaTar	danger
لا يقف في ...	laa yaqif fee ...	does not stop in ...
للمدخنين	li al-mudakhineen	smoking
لغير المدخنين	li-ghayr al-mudakhineen	non-smoking
مدخل	madkhal	entrance
محطة نهائية	maHaTTa nihaa'iya	terminus
محطة الحافلات	maHaTTat al-Haafilaat	bus station
محجوز	maHjooz	reserved
مخرج	makhraj	exit
مكتب حجز	maktab Hajz	ticket office
التذاكر	at-tazaakir	
ممنوع الدخول	mamnooA ad-dukhool	no entry
مشغول	mashghool	engaged

GETTING AROUND

موقف الباص	mowqif al-baaS	bus stop
موقف السيارات	mowqif as-sayyaaraat	car park
موقف التاكسيات	mowqif at-taksiyaat	taxi rank
قف	qef	stop
سلسلة لتوقيف القطار	selsela li towqeef al-qitaar	passenger alarm
تحويلة	taHweela	diversion
تكييف الهواء	takyeef al-hawaa'	air conditioning
وسط المدينة	wasaT al-madeena	city centre

SHOPPING

carrier bag	kees	كيس
cashdesk	khazeena	خزينة
cheap	rakheeS	رخيص
cheque	sheek	شيك
department	qism	قسم
expensive	ghaali	غالي
market	sooq	سوق
pay	dafaA	دفع
receipt	eeSaal	إيصال
shop	dukkaan	دكان
shop assistant	(m) baa'iA	بائع
	(f) baa'iAa	بائعة
supermarket	soobermaarkit	سوبرماركت

I'd like ...
ureed ...

أريد ...

have you got ...?
Aindek ...?

عندك ... ؟

how much is this?
bikam haaza?

بكم هنا ؟

**the price is too high, take
off 10%!**
ath-thaman ghaali katheer,
ekhSum Aashra fi al-mi'a!

الثمن غالي كثير ، إخصم
عشرة في المئة !

that's too expensive
haaza ghaali katheer

هذا غالي كثير

38

SHOPPING

how about ... Dinar/pounds?
eesh teqool tibeeA bi ...
deenaar/jenayh?

إيش تقول تبيع
بـ ... دينار / جنيه ؟

do you take credit cards?
mumkin adfaA bi
biTaaqat iAtimaad?

ممكن ادفع ببطاقة اعتماد ؟

could I have a receipt please?
aATeeni eeSaal, min faDlek

أعطيني إيصال ، من فضلك

I'd like to try it on
mumkin ajarrib?

ممكن أجرب ؟

I'll come back
Ha arjaA

حارجع

it's too big/small
kabeer/Sagheer

كبير / صغير

it's not what I'm looking for
moo munaasib

مو مناسب

I'll take it
Ha-ashtareeh

حاشتريه

can you gift-wrap it?
ureedu li-hadiya, mumkin
tiliffu kwaiys?

اريده لهدية ، ممكن تلفه
كويس ؟

SHOPPING

جزار	jazz**aar**	**butcher's**
خياط	khay**aa**T	**tailor**
مفتوح	maf**too**h	**open**
مخبز	makhbaz	**bakery**
مكتبة	maktaba	**bookshop**
مغلق	mughlaq	**closed**
قسم النساء	qism an-nisaa'	**ladies' department**
قسم الرجال	qism ar-rijaal	**menswear department**
سوبرماركيت	soobermaarkeet	**supermarket**
سوق	sooq	**market, bazaar**

THINGS ARABIC

RELIGION AND CUSTOMS

Since religion dominates all aspects of Arab life, some things that are perfectly ordinary behaviour in the West are considered taboo in Arab countries. It is not always easy to tell how an Arab would react to alcoholic drinks being consumed in his presence or to his sister being invited for a dance by a stranger. For obvious reasons, circumspection is also advisable when engaging in discussions involving politics. Even in the relatively 'Westernised' Arab countries which have nightclubs, alcoholic drinks, cinemas etc, discretion is advisable in contacts with local people.

Arab countries which are heavily dependent on tourism make greater efforts to accommodate the wishes and tastes of foreign visitors. In the oil-rich Arab countries, however, no such compromises are made. Strict observance of the local customs is the safest course of action, whatever the purpose of the visit.

The main religious events are as follows:

End of Ramadan	Aeed al-fiTr	عيد الفطر
Feast of the Sacrifice	Aeed al-'aDHa	عيد الأضحى

The latter occurs about two months after the end of Ramadan. It is also the period during which Muslims perform the pilgrimage to Mecca.

The Prophet's Birthday	mowlid an-nabi	مولد النبي

This is not necessarily a holiday in many Arab countries.

Ramadan	ramaDaan	رمضان

Normal social activities usually slow down in the daytime during the month of Ramadan. At night, however, a festive atmosphere prevails throughout the month. Working hours are usually reduced by up to four hours. This, however, varies widely from one country to another.

The month of Ramadan is not the best time for a businessman to visit an Arab country, as not much serious work actually gets done. In Arab countries where alcohol consumption and night clubs are usually allowed, it is advisable to show a certain degree of sensitivity to the fact that the person serving alcohol may be a devout Muslim who would rather not even set eyes on alcohol during what is for him the most sacred month, let alone serve it to a customer.

WOMEN IN THE ARAB WORLD

As with most stereotypes, commonly accepted ideas about the position of women in Arab society are, albeit in varying degrees, exaggerated. It is true to say, however, that certain freedoms taken for granted in the West are not always available to Arab women. Sometimes, such freedoms are not even actively sought. Arab women's dress varies from country to country. Some adhere strictly to the principle of veiling known as 'Hijaab' and, in the Gulf and Egypt, are covered from head to foot in black 'abayas'. In Syria and the Levant (the area including the Lebanon, Jordan, Syria, Iraq and Palestine/Israel), the women wear drab grey or brown overcoats and, in the countries of North Africa, they wear white or light brown sheets or hooded coats known as 'jellabas'. Some Arab women wear Western clothes but they take care that necklines are not too low and and that skirts are not too short.

For a Western woman visiting an Arab country, a number of aspects of life may seem strange and anachronistic. It should be remembered that cultural differences are most pronounced where the sexes, their attitudes and their respective roles in society are concerned. That Arab men view Western women as easy prey is no secret. What is perhaps not so familiar is that such attitudes are conveniently explained - even by Arab men who could be expected to know better - by reference to the way Western women are depicted in films and magazines.

Bear in mind the following 'do's' and 'don'ts':

- avoid direct eye contact when talking to men
- only shake hands when a man extends his hand first; the hand-shake may be vigorous, but it should be brief
- in mixed company, stick with the other women in the group, however boring this may seem
- bare arms, bare legs, and low necklines are seen as a deliberate flaunting of attractions; modest attire, especially for women travelling on their own, is much safer and less likely to lead to unpleasant misunderstandings
- in countries where swimming by women is allowed (for example, Tunisia), ordinary swimwear is perfectly acceptable, but elsewhere more conservative swimwear or other clothing will be safer.

DRESS

The Arab world is a man's world. There are hardly any restrictions that apply to the way men should be dressed, whether Arab or Western. It's acceptable to wear shorts on the beach and in areas geared towards Western tourism, but this is not recommended in other areas.

ARAB ETIQUETTE

The Arabs are celebrated for their hospitality and when invited to visit an Arab family, it is the done thing to take a present and offer it to the host. Do not, however, be surprised if the present is not unwrapped there and then or if the customary expressions of gratitude are barely audible. Presents are gratefully but discreetly accepted and are not opened until after the guests have left.

In many countries of the Gulf, shoes are removed at the doorstep of the house or before entering the living room, which is usually carpeted. It is polite to make this gesture but, if you know you have a hole in your socks or that they need a wash, keeping your shoes on will be the lesser of two faux-pas.

Using a knife and fork to eat may be common in some Arab countries (the Levant in particular), but most families still eat with their hands, often from the same dish. It is therefore particularly important to be seen to have washed your hands before starting to eat. Only the right hand is used for eating. However, if you are left-handed and can't manage any other way, your apologies will be appreciated.

However ravenous you may be and however delicious the particular dish in front of you, it is good manners not to leave common dishes empty. Remember that in the women's or servants' quarters, there are people who probably have to wait for the guests' table to be cleared before they can eat.

SHOPPING

A characteristic aspect of Arab life, the traditional market place or 'sooq' is to be found wherever you go in the Arab world. It is not just a place where goods are bought and sold but also a cultural institution which serves as a meeting place, a reliable source of information on local family alliances and disputes, political trends, the latest fashions etc.

The activity of buying and selling which takes place in the 'sooq' is as much social as commercial. A satisfactory transaction is one where both the buyer and the seller part company feeling they have concluded a good deal. It is in this context that bargaining and haggling over prices should best be seen. Although, as a foreigner, you might not be linguistically equipped to be witty and persuasive, appropriate body language can equally well convey your assessment of the true value of what you want to buy. Many visitors to the Arab world give the game away when looking for souvenirs by openly expressing pleasure or admiration at the sight of local artefacts. An air of studied detachment is usually more conducive to getting the shop or stall owner to pitch his opening bid somewhere between 50% and 75% above what he really expects. Note that it is not customary to bargain in larger shops that have prices displayed.

Items that will be of particular interest to Western tourists are: jewellery, crafts, gold, silver and copper-ware, rugs, brocades, antiques, ivory, enamelware and spices.

PUNCTUALITY

The concept of time is not perceived in the same way by all cultures. Punctuality is not a very highly prized virtue in the Arab world. People don't mean to keep you waiting but there are just so many other things to attend to. The infuriating word 'bukra' (tomorrow) often simply means 'not now': it may indeed mean 'tomorrow', but it may also be as indefinite as next week or next month. The expression 'inshaa'a al-laah' (God willing) is tagged on to many expressions involving future undertakings as a useful hedge against unexpected events which may make a promise impossible to keep.

ADDRESSING PEOPLE AND CONVERSATION

Age, status and power are extremely important in the Arab world. When addressing someone who is visibly older, it is not uncommon for a man to be addressed as 'sheikh' or 'Aamm' (sheik or uncle) and for a woman to be addressed as 'khaala' or 'Aamma' (both meaning aunt). Equals address each other by 'yaa sayyid ...' 'yaa sayyida ...', or 'yaa aanisa ...' (Mr, Mrs and Miss respectively), followed by the person's first name. Thus, if your name happens to be John Smith, you will be addressed as 'yaa sayyid John'.

In poorer Arab countries, an otherwise enjoyable visit may be marred by the incessant attention of beggars and self-appointed guides. Such unwelcome attention

45

can usually be discouraged by using a few well-rehearsed and firmly delivered set phrases like:

al-lah yijeeb	**God will provide**	*(to a beggar)*
laa, shukran	**no, thanks**	*(to a self-appointed guide)*

LANGUAGE

Arabic belongs to the Semitic group of languages. There are three types of Arabic: classical Arabic, Standard Literary Arabic and spoken Arabic. Classical Arabic is the Arabic in which the Koran was written and it is not used in everyday speech. Standard Literary Arabic is used in newspapers, for radio and television broadcasts and is understood by Arabic-speakers of all countries. Spoken Arabic varies from country to country, so if, say, Arabic-speakers from the Gulf and North Africa wanted to communicate, they would most probably use Standard Literary Arabic. The Arabic and pronunciation in this phrase book is a blend of Standard Literary Arabic and some universally accepted spoken Arabic words and should enable you to make yourself understood wherever you are.

MONEY

bank	bank	بنك
bill	Hisaab	حساب
bureau de change	maktab as-Saraafa	مكتب الصرافة
change *(small)*	fakka	فكة
cheque	sheek	شيك
credit card	biTaaqat iAtimaad	بطاقة اعتماد
exchange rate	siAr as-Sarf	سعر الصرف
expensive	ghaali	غالي
pounds *(sterling)*	junayh istarleeni	جنيه استرليني
price	siAr	سعر
receipt	eeSaal	إيصال
traveller's cheque	sheek siyaaHi	شيك سياحي

how much is it?
bikam?

بكم ؟

I'd like to change this into ...
ureed aghayyir haaza ilaa ...

أريد أغير هذا الى ...

can you give me something smaller?
Aindek fakka?

عندك فكة ؟

can I use this credit card?
mumkin adfaA bi-haaz al-biTaaqa?

ممكن أدفع بهذه البطاقة ؟

MONEY

can I/we have the bill please?
al-Hisaab, min faDlek

الحساب ، من فضلك

please keep the change
khood al-baaqi

خود الباقي

I think the figures are wrong
feeh ghalaT fi al-Hisaab,
aZunn

فيه غلط في الحساب، أظن

I'm completely skint
maa Aindi wa laa milleem

ما عندي و لا مليم

Each Arab country has its own currency:

Algeria	1 dinar	= 100 centimes
Bahrain	1 dinar	= 1,000 fils
Egypt	1 pound	= 100 piastres
Emirates	1 dirham	= 100 fils
Iraq	1 dinar	= 1,000 fils
Jordan	1 dinar	= 1,000 fils
Kuwait	1 dinar	= 1,000 fils
Lebanon	1 pound	= 100 piastres
Libya	1 dinar	= 1,000 dirhams
Mauritania	1 ouguiya	= 5 khoums
Morocco	1 dirham	= 100 centimes
Oman	1 riyal	= 1,000 baisa
Qatar	1 riyal	= 100 dirhams
Saudi Arabia	1 riyal	= 100 halalas
Somalia	1 shilin	= 100 cents
Sudan	1 pound	= 100 piastres
Syria	1 pound	= 100 piastres
Tunisia	1 dinar	= 1,000 millimes
Yemen	1 riyal	= 100 fils
	1 dinar	= 1,000 fils

MONEY

بنك	bank	**bank**
مكتب الصرافة	maktab as-Saraafa	**bureau de change**
ساعات العمل	saaAaat al-Aamal	**opening hours**
شيكات سياحية	sheekaat siyaaHiya	**traveller's cheques**
سعر التحويل	siAr at-taHweel	**exchange rate**

BUSINESS

business	aAmaal	أعمال
business card	kaart	كارت
company	sharika	شركة
contract	Aaqd	عقد
fax (noun)	faaks	فاكس
instalment	qisT	قسط
invoice	faatoora	فاتورة
managing director	mudeer Aamm	مدير عام
meeting	'ijtimaaA	إجتماع
price	siAr	سعر
quote (noun)	tasAeer	تسعير
target	hadaf	هدف
telex	teleks	تليكس
workflow schedule	barnaamaj sayr al-Aamal	برنامج سير العمل

I have a meeting with Mr ...
Aindi meeAaad maAa
as-sayyid ...

عندي ميعاد مع السيد ...

may I introduce Mr ...?
mumkin aAarrifek Aala
as-sayyid ...

ممكن أعرفك على السيد ...

he is our technical director/
sales director
huwwa al-mudeer at-tiqnee/
mudeer al-mabeeAaat fi
ash-sharika

هو المدير التقني / مدير
المبيعات في الشركة

BUSINESS

can we send you faxes in English?
mumkin narsil faaks bi al-ingleezi?

ممكن نرسل فاكس بالانجليزي ؟

I'd like to have time to think it over
aHtaaj shwayya waqt afakker fi al-mowDooA

أحتاج شوية وقت أفكر في الموضوع

we're very excited about it
iHna muhtammeen katheer

احنا مهتمين كثير

I'm afraid this is still a problem
li al-'asaf, lissa feeh mushkil

للأسف، لسة فيه مشكل

ok, that's a deal
Tayyib, iHna 'ettafaqna

طيب، إحنا اتفقنا

I look forward to a successful partnership
mushaaraka naajiHa, in shaa' allah

مشاركة ناجحة ، إن شاء الله

it's a pleasure doing business with you
ihna murtaaHeen li maAak at-taAaamul

إحنا مرتاحين للتعامل معك

ENTERTAINMENT

band *(pop)*	firqa	فرقة
cinema	seenima	سينما
concert	Hafla	حفلة
disco	diskoo	ديسكو
film	feelm	فيلم
go out	kharaj	خرج
music	mooseeqa	موسيقى
play *(theatre)*	masraHiya	مسرحية
seat	maqAad	مقعد
show	sahra	سهرة
singer	*(m)* mughanni	مغني
	(f) mughanniya	مغنية
theatre	masraH	مسرح
ticket	tazkira	تذكرة

**are you doing anything
tonight?** *(to a man/woman)*
inta mashghool/inti
mashghoola al-layla?

إنت مشغول / إنت مشغولة
الليلة ؟

**do you want to come out with
me tonight?**
tureed nukhruj maAa baAD,
al-layla?

تريد نخرج مع بعض،
الليلة ؟

what's on in the cinema?
eesh fi as-seenima al-yowm?

إيش في السينما اليوم ؟

ENTERTAINMENT

which is the best disco round here?
feen aHsan diskoo, hina?

فين أحسن ديسكو ، هنا ؟

let's go to the cinema/theatre
ya-llah nimshi li as-seenima/li al-masraH

يا الله نمشي للسينما / للمسرح

I've seen it
shuftu min qabl

شفته من قبل

I'll meet you at 9 o'clock at the station
niltaqee fi as-saaAa tisAa fi al-maHaTTa

نلتقي في الساعة تسعة في المحطة

can I have two tickets for tonight?
tazkirathayn li al-yowm fi al-layl, min faDlek

تذكرتين لليوم في الليل ، من فضلك

I'd like to book three seats for tomorrow
ureed aHjez thalaath maqaaAid li-bukra

أريد أحجز ثلاث مقاعد لبكرة

let's go out for some fresh air
ya-llah, nukhruj barra, neshim al-hawa

يا الله نخرج برة ، نشم الهواء

will you let me back in again later?
mumkin akhruj wa arjaA?

ممكن أخرج و أرجع ؟

I'm meeting someone inside
Aindee meeAaad maAa Sadeeq hinaak

عندي ميعاد مع صديق هناك

ENTERTAINMENT

مكتب حجز	maktab Hajz	booking office
ملهى	malhaa	amusement centre
مركز الرياضة	markaz ar-riyaaDa	sports centre
مسرح	masraH	theatre
نادي ليلي	naadee laylee	night club
سينما	seenima	cinema

THE BEACH

beach	shaaTi'	شاطىء
beach umbrella	shamsiya	شمسية
bikini	bikeeni	بكيني
dive	ghaTas	غطس
sand	raml	رمل
sea	baHr	بحر
sunbathe	tashammas	تشمس
suntan lotion	kreem Didd ash-shams	كريم ضد الشمس
suntan oil	zayt Didd ash-shams	زيت ضد الشمس
swim	sabaH	سبح
swimming costume	maayoo	مايو
tan (verb)	samura	سمر
towel	fooTa	فوطة
wave	mowja	موجة

let's go down to the beach
ya-llah nemshi li shaaTi' al-baHr

يا الله نمشي لشاطىء البحر

what's the water like?
al-moya, kayf?

المويا ، كيف ؟

it's freezing
zayy ath-thalj

زي الثلج

it's beautiful
al-moya daafi'a

المويا دافئة

THE BEACH

are you coming for a swim?	taAaala tesbaH	تعالى تسبح
I can't swim	maa aArif asbaH	ما اعرف أسبح
he swims like a fish	huwwa sabbaaH baariA	هو سباح بارع
will you keep an eye on my things for me?	mumkin teraaAi amtiAati?	ممكن تراعي أمتعتي ؟
is it deep here?	Aameeq hina?	عميق هنا ؟
I'm all sunburnt	'iHtaraqt bi ash-shams katheer	احترقت بالشمس كثير
you're all wet!	shoof kayf inta muballal!	شوف كيف انت مبلل !
let's go up to the café	ya-llah nimshee li al-maqha	يا الله نمشي للمقهى

الـعاب الكرة	alAaab al-kora	no ball games
ممنوعة	mamnooAa	
دوش	doosh	shower
خاص	khaaS	private
خطر	khaTar	danger
للإيجار	li al-'eejaar	for hire
ممنوع الغطس	mamnooA al-ghaTs	no diving
ممنوع السباحة	mamnooA as-sibaaHa	no swimming

56

PROBLEMS

accident	Haadith	حادث
ambulance	sayyaarat 'isAaaf	سيارة إسعاف
broken	mukassar	مكسر
doctor	Tabeeb	طبيب
emergency	Tawaari'	طوارئ
fire	Hareeq	حريق
fire brigade	Rijaal al-'iTfa'	رجال الأطفاء
ill	mareeD	مريض
injured	muSaab bi jurooH	مصاب بجروح
late	muta'akhir	متأخر
out of order	kharbaan	خربان
police	ash-shorTa	الشرطة

can you help me? I'm lost
mumkin tisaaAidni? DaiyaAt at-Tareeq

ممكن تساعدني ؟ ضيعت الطريق

I've lost my passport
DaiyaAt al-jowaaz

ضيعت الجواز

I've locked myself out of my room
maa aqdar adkhul, nasayt al-miftaaH daakhil al-ghurfa

ما أقدر أدخل، نسيت المفتاح داخل الغرفة

my luggage hasn't arrived
Haqaa'ibi maa waSalat

حقائبي ما وصلت

I can't get it open
maa aqdar aftaHu

ما أقدر أفتحه

PROBLEMS

it's jammed
maa aqdar aftaHu

ما اقدر أفتحه

I don't have enough money
maa Aindi fuloos kaafiya

ما عندي فلوس كافية

I've broken down
sayyaarati kharbaana

سيارتي خربانة

this is an emergency
haazi Haalat Tawaari'

هذه حالة طوارء

help!
al-'ighaatha!

الإغاثة !

it doesn't work
kharbaan

خربان

the lights aren't working in my room
al-lambaat fi ghurfati moo shaghaala

اللمبات في غرفتي مو شغالة

the lift is stuck
al-mesAad kharbaan

المصعد خربان

I can't understand a single word
maa fahimt wa laa kilma

ما فهمت و لا كلمة

can you get an interpreter?
feeh aHad yitarjim?

فيه أحد يترجم ؟

the toilet won't flush
maa feeh moya li shaTf at-twalet

ما فيه مويا لشطف التواليت

there's no plug in the bath
maa feeh saddaada fi al-Hammaam

ما فيه سدادة في الحمام

58

PROBLEMS

there's no hot water
maa feeh moya sukhna

ما فيه مويا سخنة

there's no toilet paper left
al-waraq khallaS fi twalet

الورق خلص في التواليت

I'm afraid I've accidentally broken the ...
ana aasif, laakin kassart ...

انا آسف ، لاكن كسرت ...

this man has been following me
Haaz ar-rajul yamshi khalfi min mudda

هذا الرجل يمشي خلفي من مدة

I've been mugged
eAtudiya Aalayy wa 'tsaraqt

أعتدي علي و اتسرقت

my handbag has been stolen
shanTeti ensaraqat

شنطتي انسرقت

عاطل	AaaTil	**out of order**
الشرطة	as-shorTa	**police**
إسعافات أولية	isAaafaat awwaliya	**first aid**
خطر	khaTar	**danger**
مخرج الطوارىء	makhraj at-Tawaari'	**emergency exit**
رجال الأطفاء	Rijaal al-'iTfa'	**fire brigade**
صيدلية	Saydaliya	**chemist's**
سيارة إسعاف	sayyaarat 'isAaaf	**ambulance**
طوارىء	Tawaari'	**emergency**

59

HEALTH

bandage	rabbaaTa	رباطة
blood	damm	دم
broken	maksoor	مكسور
burn	Harq	حرق
chemist's	Saydaliya	صيدلية
contraception	manA al-Haml	منع الحمل
dentist	Tabeeb al-asnaan	طبيب الأسنان
disabled	muqAad	مقعد
disease	maraD	مرض
doctor	Tabeeb	طبيب
health	SiHHa	صحة
hospital	mustashfa	مستشفى
ill	mareeD	مريض
nurse	mumarriDa	ممرضة
wound	jurH	جرح

I don't feel well
ana taAbaan

أنا تعبان

it's getting worse
aHiss inni aswa'

أحس اني أسوء

I feel better
ana aHsan, al-Hamdu li-laah

أنا أحسن ، الحمد لله

I'm going to be sick
ureed astafrigh

اريد استفرغ

I've got a pain here
Aindi wajaA hina

عندي وجع هنا

60

HEALTH

it hurts
yoojaAni

يوجعني

he's got a high temperature
feeh Humma

فيه حمى

could you call a doctor?
mumkin tittaSil bi Tabeeb?

ممكن تتصل بطبيب ؟

is it serious?
al-Haala khaTira?

الحالة خطرة ؟

will he need an operation?
laazim Aamaliya?

لازم عملية ؟

I'm diabetic
Aindi maraD as-sukkar

عندي مرض السكر

keep her warm
ghaTTeeha kwayis

غطيها كويس

have you got anything for ...?
ureed dowaa' Didd ...

اريد دواء ضد ...

عيادة	Aiyaada	clinic
غرفة الإنتظار	ghurfat al-'intiZaar	waiting room
إسعافات أولية	isAaafaat awwaliya	first aid
مركز	markaz SiHHee	health centre
مستشفى	mustashfa	hospital
صيدلية	Saydaliya	chemist's
طبيب	Tabeeb	doctor
طبيب الأسنان	Tabeeb al-asnaan	dentist
طوارىء	Tawaari'	emergencies

61

SPORT

which team is winning?
man al-fareeq al-faa'iz?

من الفريق الفائز ؟

I want to learn to sailboard
ureed atAallam arkub lowH
shuraaAee

أريد أتعلم أركب لوح شراعي

can we hire a sailing boat?
mumkin nista'jir qaarib
shuraaAee?

ممكن نستأجر قارب
شراعي ؟

how much is half an hour's waterskiing?
bikam nuS saaAa min
al-inzilaaq Aala SaTH
al-maa'?

بكم نص ساعة من الإنزلاق
على سطح الماء ؟

can we use the tennis court?
mumkin nistaAmil malAab
at-tinees?

ممكن نستعمل ملعب
التنيس ؟

I'd like to go and watch a football match
ureed arooH atfarraj fi
mubaarat korat al-qadam

أريد أروح أتفرج في مباراة
كرة القدم

is there any camel-racing this week?
feeh sibaaq al-jamal haaz
al-usbooA?

فيه سباق الجمل هذا
الأسبوع ؟

we'd like to see some horse-racing
nureed neshaahid sibaaq
al-khayl

نريد نشاهد سباق الخيل

THE POST OFFICE

letter	khiTaab	خطاب
post office	maktab al-bareed	مكتب البريد
recorded delivery	khiTaab musajjal	خطاب مسجل
send	rasal	رسل
stamp	TaabeA	طابع
telegram	barqiya	برقية

how much is a letter to Ireland?
bikam irsaal khiTaab li irlanda?

بكم إرسال خطاب لإرلندا ؟

I'd like four ... stamps
aATeeni arbaAa TowaabiA li ..., min faDlek

اعطيني أربعة طوابع ل .... ، من فضلك

I'd like six stamps for postcards to England
ureed sitta TowaabiA biTaaqaat bareediya li inglaterra

أريد ستة طوابع بطاقات بريدية لإنجلترا

is there any mail for me?
feeh khiTaabaat lee?

فيه خطابات لي ؟

I'm expecting a parcel from ...
atawaqqaA Tard min ...

أتوقع طرد من ...

THE POST OFFICE

البريد العادي	al-bareed al-Aaadee	surface mail
البريد الجوي	al-bareed al-jawwee	air mail
مكتب البريد	maktab al-bareed	post office
أوقات جمع	owqaat jamA	collection times
الرسائل	ar-rasaa'il	
تلغرافات	teleghraafaat	telegrams
طرود	Turood	parcels

TELEPHONING

directory enquiries	'istiAlaamaat	إستعلامات
engaged	mashghool	مشغول
extension	farA	فرع
number	raqm	رقم
operator	muwaZZaf	موظف
phone (verb)	'ittaSal	إتصل
phone box	tilifoon Aumoomi	تليفون عمومي
telephone	tilifoon	تلفون
telephone directory	daleel al-haatif	دليل الهاتف

is there a phone round here?
feeh tilifoon hina?

فيه تلفون هنا ؟

can I use your phone?
mumkin astaAmil at-tilifoon?

ممكن أستعمل التلفون ؟

I'd like to make a phone call to Britain
ureed attaSil bi inglaterra

أريد أتصل بإنجلترا

I want to reverse the charges
ureed taHweel taklifat al-mukaalama

أريد تحويل تكلفة المكالمة

hello
aaloo

آلو

could I speak to Ahmed?
aHmed, min faDlek

أحمد ، من فضلك

TELEPHONING

hello, this is Simon speaking
aaloo, haaza 'Simon'

آلو، هذا سايمن

could you tell him that ...?
mumkin tiqool lu ...?

ممكن تقول له ... ؟

do you speak English?
titkallam ingleezi?

تتكلم إنجليزي ؟

could you say that again very very slowly?
aAid kilma bi kilma, wa laa tisraA, min faDlek

أعد كلمة بكلمة، و لا تسرع، من فضلك

could you tell him Jim called?
mumkin tiqool lu 'Jim' ittaSal?

ممكن تقول له دجيم إتصل ؟

could you ask her to ring me back?
qool laha tittaSil bee, low samaHt

قول لها تتصل بي، لو سمحت

I'll call back later
Ha-'attaSil marra thaaniya

حاتصل مرة ثانية

my number is ...
raqm tilifooni huwa ...

رقم تلفوني هو ...

76 32 11
sitta wa sabAeen ithnayn wa thalaatheen iHda-Aashar

ستة و سبعين   إثنين و
ثلاثين   إحدى عشر

just a minute, please
laHZa, low samaHt

لحظة، لو سمحت

he's not in
huwa moo mowjood

هو مو موجود

66

TELEPHONING

sorry, I've got the wrong
number
aasif, ar-raqm ghalaT

آسف ، الرقم غلط

it's a terrible line
al-khaTT moo kwayis

الخط مو كويس

REPLIES

لا تقطع ، لو سمحت | laa tiqTaA, low samaHt
hang on

من يتكلم ؟ | man yatkallam?
who's calling?

عاطل عن العمل	AaaTil Aan al-Aamal	out of order
هاتف	haatif	telephone
استعلامات	'istiAlaamaat	directory enquiries
اتصال مباشر	'ittiSaal mubaashir	direct dialling
مكالمة دولية	mukaalamaat dowliya	international calls
مكالمات محلية	mukaalamaat maHalliya	local calls
طوارىء	Tawaari'	emergency
تلفون	tilifoon	telephone

NUMBERS, THE DATE AND THE TIME

Note that the countries of North Africa (Morocco, Algeria, Tunisia and Libya) all use Western figures but the pronunciation is the same as for all Arab countries.

	number		figure in words
0	Sifr	.	صفر
1	waaHid	١	واحد
2	'ithnayn	٢	إثنين
3	thalaatha	٣	ثلاثة
4	arbaAa	٤	أربعة
5	khamsa	٥	خمسة
6	sitta	٦	ستة
7	sabAa	٧	سبعة
8	thamaaniya	٨	ثمانية
9	tisAa	٩	تسعة
10	Aashara	١٠	عشرة
11	iHda-Aashar	١١	إحدى عشر
12	ithna-Aashar	١٢	إثنا عشر
13	thalaatha-Aashar	١٣	ثلاثة عشر
14	arbaAta-Aashar	١٤	أربعة عشر
15	khamsata-Aashar	١٥	خمسة عشر
16	sittata-Aashar	١٦	ستة عشر
17	sabAata-Aashar	١٧	سبعة عشر
18	thamaaniyata-Aashar	١٨	ثمانية عشر
19	tisAata-Aashar	١٩	تسعة عشر
20	Aishreen	٢٠	عشرين
21	waaHid wa Aishreen	٢١	واحد و عشرين
22	ithnayn wa Aishreen	٢٢	إثنين و عشرين
30	thalaatheen	٣٠	ثلاثين

NUMBERS, THE DATE AND THE TIME

35	khamsa wa thalaatheen	٣٥	خمسة و ثلاثين
40	arbaAeen	٤٠	أربعين
50	khamseen	٥٠	خمسين
60	sitteen	٦٠	ستين
70	sabAeen	٧٠	سبعين
80	thamaaneen	٨٠	ثمانين
90	tisAeen	٩٠	تسعين
91	waaHid wa tisAeen	٩١	واحد و تسعين
100	mi'a	١٠٠	مائة
101	mi'a wa waaHid	١٠١	مائة و واحد
200	mi'atayn	٢٠٠	مائتين
202	mi'atayn wa ithnayn	٢٠٢	مائتين و إثنين
1,000	alf	١٠٠٠	ألف
2,000	alfayn	٢٠٠٠	ألفين
1,000,000	milyoon	١٠٠٠٠٠٠	مليون

1st	al-awwal	الأول
2nd	ath-thaani	الثاني
3rd	ath-thaalith	الثالث
4th	ar-raabiA	الرابع
5th	al-khaamis	الخامس
6th	as-saadis	السادس
7th	as-saabiA	السابع
8th	ath-thaamin	الثامن
9th	at-taasiA	التاسع
10th	al-Aaashir	العاشر

NUMBERS, THE DATE AND THE TIME

what's the date?
eesh taareekh al-yowm?

إيش تاريخ اليوم ؟

it's the first of June
al-yowm Awwal yoonyu

اليوم أول يونيو

it's the tenth/twelfth of May 1994
al-yowm Aashra/ithna-Aashar
maayoo alf wa tisAu mi'a
wa arbaAa wa tisAeen

اليوم عشرة / إثنا عشر ماير
ألف و تسع مائة
و أربعة و تسعين

what time is it?
as-saaAa kam?

الساعة كم ؟

it's midday/midnight
aZ-Zuhr/nuS al-layl

الظهر / نص الليل

it's one/three o'clock
as-saaAa waHda/thalaatha

الساعة وحدة / ثلاثة

it's twenty past three/twenty to three
as-saaAa thalaatha wa thulth/
thalaatha illa thulth

الساعة ثلاثة و
ثلث / ثلاثة إلا ثلث

it's half past eight
as-saaAa thamaaniya wa nuS

الساعة ثمانية و نص

it's a quarter past/a quarter to five
as-saaAa khamsa wa
rubA'/khamsa illa rubA'

الساعة خمسة
و ربع / خمسة إلا ربع

at two/five pm
fi as-saaAa ithnayn/khamsa
baAda aZ-Zuhr

في الساعة إثنين /
خمسة بعد الظهر

Under each verb two forms are given: the first is the perfect form and the second the imperfect; see also grammar.

A	**age**	عمر
	Aumr	
	agent	وكيل
	wakeel	
a	**ago: three days**	من قبل ثلاثة
(see grammar)	**ago**	أيام
about *(approx)* تقريبا	min qabl	
taqreeban	thalaathat ayaam	
above *(prep)* فوق	**agree: I agree**	متفق
fowq	muttafiq	
accident حادث	**Aids**	مرض الايدز
Haadith	maraD al-aydz	
adaptor	**air**	هواء
(for voltage) محول	hawa	
muHawwil	**air-conditioning**	مكيف
(plug) وصيلة	mukayyif	
waSeela	**airmail: by**	
address عنوان	**airmail**	بريد جوي
Aunwaan	bareed jawwee	
adult بالغ	**airport**	مطار
baaligh	maTaar	
aeroplane طائرة	**alarm clock**	منبه
Taa'ira	munabbih	
after بعد	**alcohol**	كحول
baAd	kuHool	
afternoon بعد الظهر	**Algeria**	الجزائر
baAd aZ-Zuhr	al-jazaa'ir *(f)*	
afterwards بعدين	**alive**	حي
baAdeen	Hayy	
again مرة ثانية	**all**	كل
marra thaaniya	kull	
against ضد	**Allah**	الله
Didd	allah	

English	Arabic	English	Arabic
allergic to ...	حساسية	**antibiotic**	مضاد للجراثم
Hasaasiya li ...	... ل	mudaaD li	
allowed	مسموح	al-jaraathim	
masmooH		**antihistamine**	دواء ضد
all right: that's		dawaa' Didd	الحساسية
all right	طيب	al-Hasaasiya	
Tayyib		**antiseptic**	مانع للعفونة
almost	تقريبا	maaniA li	
taqreeban		al-Aufoona	
alone	لوحدي	**apartment**	شقة
li-waHdi		shaqqa	
also	كمان	**appendicitis**	الزائدة
kamaan		az-zaa'ida	
altogether	الكل	**apple**	تفاحة
al-kull		tuffaaHa	
always	دائما	**appointment**	موعد
daa'iman		mawAid	
ambulance	سيارة إسعاف	**apricot**	مشمش
sayyaarat		meshmesh	
'isAaf		**April**	إبريل
America	أمريكا	abreel	
amreeka		**Arab** (adj)	عربي
amp: 13-amp	ثلاثة عشر	Aarabee	
thalaatha-Aashar		(man)	عربي
amber	أمبير	Arabbee	
and	و	(woman)	عربية
wa		Aarabiya	
angry	زعلان	**Arabian Gulf**	
zaAlaan		al-khaleej	الخليج العربي
ankle	كاحل	al-Aarabee	
kaaHil		**Arabic**	
another		al-lugha	اللغة العربية
(different)		al-Aarabiya	
aakhar (m)	آخر	**arm**	ذراع
ukhra (f)	أخرى	ziraA	
another beer		**arrest**	يقبض على
beera thaaniya	بيرة ثانية	qabaD Aala	
answer	جواب	**arrive**	يصل
jawaab		waSal,	يصل
		yaSil	

72

English	Arabic
art	فن
fann	
artist	فنان
fannaan	
ashtray	منفضة سجاير
minfaDat	
sejaayir	
ask	سأل
sa'al,	
yis'al	يسأل
asleep	نائم
naa'im	
aspirin	أسبرين
'asbireen	
asthma	مرض الربو
maraD ar-rabuw	
at: at the station	في المحطة
fee al-maHaTTa	
at Ahmed's	عند احمد
Aind aHmed	
attractive	جناب
jazzaab	
August	أغسطس
aghosTus	
aunt *(maternal)*	خالة
khaala	
(paternal)	عمة
Aamma	
automatic	اتوماتيكي
utumateekee	
autumn	خريف
khareef	
awake	صاحي
SaaHee	
awful	قبيح
qabeeH	
axle	محور العجلة
muHawwir	
al-Aajala	

B

English	Arabic
baby	طفل
Tifl	
back	خلف
khalf	
(of body)	ظهر
Zahr	
come back	رجع
rajaA,	
yarjeA	يرجع
go back	عاد
Aad,	
ya'ood	يعود
bad	سيء
sayyi'	
bag *(carrier)*	كيس
kees	
baggage check	خزانة للشنط
(US)	
khizaana li	
ash-shonooT	
Bahrein	البحرين
al-baHrayn *(f)*	
baker	خباز
khabbaaz	
bald	أصلع
'aSlaA	
ball	كرة
kora	
banana	موز
mowz	
bandage	رباطة
rabbaata	
bank	بنك
bank	

bar	بار	**before**	قبل
baar		qabl	
barber	حلاق	**begin**	بدأ
Hallaaq		bada',	
basketball	كرة السلة	yebda'	يبدأ
korat as-salla		**behind** (prep)	خلف
bath	حمام	khalf	
Hammaam		**bell**	جرس
bathroom	حمام	jaras	
Hammaam		**belly dancing**	رقص بلدي
battery	بطارية	raqS baladee	
baTTaariya		**below** (prep)	تحت
be		taHt	
kaan,	كان	**belt**	حزام
yakoon;	يكون	Hizaam	
(see grammar)		**bend**	منعطف
beach	شاطىء البحر	munAaTaf	
shaaTi' al-baHr		**best: the best**	الأحسن
beans	فاصولية	al-aHsan;	
faaSooliya		(see grammar)	
beard	لحية	**better**	أحسن
leHya		aHsan;	
beautiful	جميل	(see grammar)	
jameel		**between** (prep)	بين
because	لأن	bayn	
lianna		**bicycle**	دراجة
bed	سرير	darraaja	
sareer		**big**	كبير
Bedouin: the		kabeer	
Bedouin	بدو	**bill**	
badw		faatoora	فاتورة
bedroom	غرفة النوم	(in restaurant)	
ghurfat an-nowm		Hisaab	حساب
bee	نحلة	**bird**	عصفور
naHla		AuSfoor	
beef	لحم البقر	**biro**(R)	قلم حبر
laHm al-baqar		qalam Hibr	
beer	بيرة	**birthday**	عيد ميلاد
beera		Aeed meelaad	

English	Arabic	English	Arabic
biscuit biskoot	بسكوت	(car) shanTat as-sayyaara	شنطة السيارة
bit: a little bit shwayya	شوية	**border** Hodood	حدود
bite (insect) ladgha	لدغة	**boring** mumill	ممل
(animal) AaDDa	عضة	**boss** mudeer	مدير
black aswad	أسود	**both: both of them** al-ithnayn maAa baAd	الإثنين مع بعض
blanket baTaaniya	بطانية		
blind aAmaa	أعمى	**bottle** zujaaja	زجاجة
blocked masdood	مسدود	**bottle-opener** fattaaHa	فتاحة
blond ashqar	أشقر	**bowl** TaaSa	طاسة
blonde shaqraa'	شقراء	**box** Sandooq	صندوق
blood damm	دم	**boy** walad	ولد
blouse blooza	بلوزة	**boyfriend** Sadeeq	صديق
blue azraq	أزرق	**bra** sutiyaan	سوتيان
boat qaarib	قارب	**bracelet** siwaar	سوار
body jism	جسم	**brakes** faraamel	فرامل
bomb qonbula	قنبلة	**brandy** braandi	براندي
bone AaZm	عظم	**brave** shujaA	شجاع
book kitaab	كتاب	**bread** khubz	خبز
bookshop maktaba	مكتبة	**break** kassar, yekasser	كسر يكسر
boot (shoe) Hezaa'	حذاء		

English	Arabic
breakfast	فطور
fuToor	
bridge (over river etc)	كبري
kubri	
briefcase	شنطة
shanTa	
bring	
jaab,	جاب
yejeeb	يجيب
Britain	بريطانيا
breTaanya	
broken	مكسر
mukassar	
brooch	بروش
broosh	
brother	أخ
akh	
brown	بني
bunnee	
brush	فرشة
forsha	
bucket	سطل
saTl	
building	بناية
binaaya	
bulb (light)	لمبة
lamba	
burn (noun)	حرق
Harq	
bus	باص
baaS	
business	أعمال
aAmaal	
business trip	رحلة عمل
riHlat Aamal	
bus station	محطة الباصات
maHaTTat al-baaSaat	

English	Arabic
bus stop	موقف الباص
mowqif al-baaS	
but	لاكن
laakin	
butcher	جزار
jazzaar	
butter	زبدة
zubda	
button	زر
zirr	
buy	
'ishtaraa,	اشترى
yashtaree	يشتري
by	ب
bi	
by car	بالسيارة
bi as-sayaara	

C

café	مقهى
maqhaa	
Cairo	القاهرة
al-qaahira	
cake	كيك
kayk	
calculator	آلة حاسبة
aala Haasiba	
calendar	يومية
yowmiya	
camel	جمل
jamal	
camera	كامرة
kamera	
can (noun)	علبة
Aulba	
can: I/she can	ممكن
mumkin	

76

ENGLISH-ARABIC

English	Arabic
I can't swim moo qaadir asbaH	مو قادر اسبح
Canada kanada	كندا
cancel algha, yulghi	ألغى يلغي
cap qubbaAa	قبعة
car sayyaara	سيارة
card (business) kart	كارت
careful: be careful! khuz baalek!	خذ بالك !
car park maHaTTat sayyaaraat	محطة سيارات
carpet sajjaada	سجادة
carrot jazar	جزر
cassette shareeT	شريط
cassette player musajjil	مسجل
cat bissa	بيسة
cauliflower qarnabeeT	قرنبيط
cave kahf	كهف
ceiling saqf	سقف
cemetery maqbara	مقبرة
centigrade daraja mi'awiya	درجة مئوية

English	Arabic
centre wasaT	وسط
certificate shahaada	شهادة
chain (around neck) silsila	سلسلة
chair kursee	كرسي
change (small) fakka	فكة
change (verb: something) ghaiyar, yeghaiyir	غير يغير
change trains ghaiyar al-qiTaar	غير القطار
cheap rakheeS	رخيص
check (US: money) sheek	شيك
check (verb) t'akkad, yet'akkad	تأكد يتأكد
check-in tasjeel al-Haqaa'ib	تسجيل الحقائب
cheers! seHHa!	صحة !
cheese jubna	جبنة
chemist Saydaliyya	صيدلية
cheque sheek	شيك
cherry karaz	كرز
chest Sadr	صدر

chewing gum	مستيكة	clock	ساعة
masteeka		saAa	
chicken	دجاج	close (verb)	
dajaaj		qafal,	قفل
(meat)	لحم دجاج	yeqfel	يقفل
laHm dajaaj		closed	مقفول
child	طفل	maqfool	
Tifl		closet (US)	دولاب
chin	ذقن	dulaab	
zaqn		clothes	ملابس
chips	بطاطة مقلية	malaabis	
baTaaTes		clothes peg	علاقة الملابس
maqliyya		Aallaaqat	
(US)	كريسبس	al-malaabis	
kreesbs		cloudy	غائم
chocolate	شكلاطة	ghaa'im	
shukulaaTa		clutch	كلاتش
Christmas	عيد الميلاد	klaatsh	السيارة
Aeed al-meelaad		as-sayyaara	
church	كنيسة	coat	بالطو
kaneesa		baalTu	
cigar	سيجار	coathanger	علاقة
seejaar		Aallaaqa	
cigarette	سيجارة	cockroach	صرصار
sijaara		SarSaar	
cinema	سينما	coffee	قهوة
seenima		qahwa	
city	مدينة	coffee house	مقهى
madeena		maqha	
city centre	وسط المدينة	cold (adj)	برد
wasaT		bard	
al-madeena		cold: I've got a	
clean (adj)	نظيف	cold	أنا مزكم
naZeef		ana muzakkam	
clean (verb)		collect call	تحويل تكلفة
naZZaf,	نظف	taHweel taklifat	التلفون
yunaZZif	ينظف	at-tilifoon	
clever	شاطر	colour	لون
shaaTer		lown	

78

colour film	فيلم ملون	correct	صحيح
feelm mulawwan		SaHeeH	
comb	مشط	cotton	قطن
mushT		quTn	
come		cotton wool	قطن طبي
jaa',	جاء	quTn Tebbee	
yajee'	يجئ	cough (noun)	سعال
come back		suAal	
rajaA,	رجع	country	بلد
yarjeA	يرجع	balad	
come in!		course: of course	طبعاً
tafaDDal!	تفضل !	TabAan	
comfortable	مريح	crab	سلطعون
mureeH		salTaAoon	
complicated	معقد	cream (to eat)	قشدة
muAaqqad		qashda	
computer	كمبيوتر	credit card	بطاقة اعتماد
kampiyooter		biTaaqat	
concert	حفلة موسيقية	'iAtimaad	
Hafla		crisps	كريسبس
mooseeqiya		kreesbs	
condom	كبوت	crocodile	تمساح
kabot		timsaaH	
congratulations!	مبروك !	crowded	مزدحم
mabrook!		muzdaHim	
constipated: I'm		cry	
constipated	عندي إمساك	bakaa,	بكى
Aindee imsaak		yabkee	يبكي
consulate	قنصلية	cup	
qunsuliya		finjaan	فنجان
contact lenses	عدسات لاصقة	cupboard	دولاب
Aadasaat		dulaab	
laaSiqa		curtain	ستارة
cool	بارد	sitaara	
baarid		Customs	جمرك
corkscrew	بريمة	jumruk	
bareema		cyclist	راكب دراجة
corner	زاوية	raakib darraaja	
zaawiya			

ENGLISH-ARABIC

D

Damascus	دمشق
dimashq (f)	
dangerous	خطير
khaTeer	
dark	ظلام
Dalaam	
date (time)	تاريخ
taareekh	
dates	ثمر
thamr	
daughter	بنت
bint (f)	
day	يوم
yowm	
dead	ميت
mayyit	
deaf	أطرش
'atrash	
death	موت
mowt	
decaffeinated	بدون كافئين
bidoon kaaf'een	
December	ديسمبر
desember	
deep	عميق
Aameeq	
delicious	لذيذ
lazeez	
dentist	طبيب الأسنان
Tabeeb al-asnaan	
deodorant	مزيل رائحة
muzeel raa'iHat	العرق
al-Aarq	
depend: it all	
depends	يمكن
yimken	

desert	صحراء
saHraa'	
dessert	دسير
diseer	
diabetic	مصاب بمرض
muSaab bi	السكر
maraD	
as-sukkar	
dialect	لهجة
lahja	
dialling code	رمز التلفون
ramz at-tilifoon	
diamond	الماس
al-maas	
diarrhoea	إسهال
ishaal	
diary	مذكرة
muzakkira	
dictionary	قاموس
qaamoos	
die	مات
maat,	
yamoot	يموت
different	مختلف
mukhtalif	
difficult	صعب
SaAb	
Dinar	دينار
deenaar	
dining room	غرفة الطعام
ghurfat	
at-TaAam	
dinner	عشاء
Aasha'	
direct	مباشر
mubaashir	
direction	اتجاه
'ittijaah	
Dirham	درهم
dirham	

dirty	وسخان	**dream**	حلم
waskhaan		Hulm	
disabled	مقعد	**dress**	فستان
muqAad		fustaan	
disaster	كارثة	**drink** *(noun)*	مشروب
kaaritha		mashroob	
disease	مرض	**drink** *(verb)*	
maraD		sharib,	شرب
disgusting	عفن	yashrab	يشرب
Aafen		**drinking water**	
disinfectant	مطهر	maa' SaaliHa li	ماء صالح
muTahhir		ash-shurb	للشرب
distance	مسافة	**drive**	
masaafa		saaq,	ساق
district *(in town)*	حي	yasooq	يسوق
Haiy		**driver**	سائق
disturb		saa'iq	
zaAaj,	زعج	**driving licence**	رخصة قيادة
yuzAij	يزعج	rokhsat qiyaada	
divorced	مطلق	**drugstore** *(US)*	صيدلية
mutallaq		Saydaliyya	
do		**drunk**	سكران
Aamal,	عمل	sakraan	
yaAmal	يعمل	**dry**	ناشف
that'll do nicely	كدى كويس	naashif	
kida kwayis		**dry-cleaner**	تنظيف على
doctor	طبيب	tanZeef Aala	الناشف
Tabeeb		an-naashif	
dog	كلب	**duck**	بطة
kalb		baTTa	
doll	دمية		
dumiya			
dollar	دولار	**E**	
doolaar			
door	باب		
baab			
down: down there	هناك تحت	**ear(s)**	أذن
hinaak taHt		'uzen	
downstairs	تحت	**early**	بدري
taHt		badri	

81

ENGLISH-ARABIC

earrings	حلقات	end (noun)	نهاية
Halaqaat		nihaaya	
earth	أرض	engaged (toilet)	مشغول
'arD (f)		mashghool	
east	شرق	(to be married)	مخطوب
sharq		makhToob	
easy	سهل	engine	محرك
sahl		muHarrik	
eat	أكل	England	إنجلترا
'akal,		inglaterra	
ya'kul	يأكل	English (language)	اللغة
egg	بيض	al-lugha	الإنجليزية
bayD		al-ingleeziya	
boiled egg	بيض مسلوق	English	
bayD maslooq		girl/woman	إنجليزية
Egypt	مصر	ingleeziya	
miSr (f)		Englishman	إنجليزي
either ... or ...	أما ... أو ...	ingleezi	
amma ... ow ...		enough	كفاية
elastic (noun)	مرن	kefaaya	
maren		that's enough	يكفي
elbow	كوع	yakfi	
KooA		entrance	مدخل
electric	كهربائي	madkhal	
kahrabaa'ee		envelope	ظرف
electricity	كهرباء	Zarf	
kahrabaa'		epileptic	صرعي
elephant	فيل	SarAee	
feel		Europe	أوربا
elevator	مصعد	oorubbaa	
miSAad		evening	المساء
else: something		al-masaa'	
else	شيء آخر	every	كل
shaiy' aakhar		kull	
embassy	سفارة	everyone	كل واحد
safaara		kull waaHid	
emergency	حالة طوارئ	everything	كل شيء
Haalat Tawaari'		kull shay'	
empty	فاضي	everywhere	كل مكان
faaDi		kull makaan	

82

ENGLISH-ARABIC

excellent	ممتاز	**factory**	مصنع
mumtaaz		maSnaA	
exchange *(verb: money)*		**family**	عائلة
		Aa'ila	
ghaiyyar,	غير	**famous**	مشهور
yughaiyer	يغير	mash-hoor	
exchange rate	سعر العملة	**fan** *(cooling)*	مروحة
siAr al-Aumla		mirwaHa	
exciting	مثير	**fantastic**	رائع
mutheer		raa'iA	
excuse me *(to get past)*	لو سمحت	**far** *(away)*	بعيد
low samaHt		baAeed	
(to get attention)	من فضلك !	**farm**	مزرعة
min faDlek!		mazraAa	
(pardon?)	إيش قلت ؟	**fashionable**	موضة
eesh qult?		mooDa	
exhibition	عرض	**fast** *(adj)*	سريع
AarD		sareeA	
exit	مخرج	**fast** *(noun: during Ramadan)*	صيام
makhraj		Siyaam	
expensive	غالي	**fast** *(verb: during Ramadan)*	
ghaali		Saam,	صام
explain	شرح	yeSoom	يصوم
sharaH,		**fat** *(person)*	سمين
yashraH	يشرح	sameen	
eye	عين	**father**	أب
Aayn		'ab	
eyes	العينين	**faucet** *(US)*	صنبور
al-Aaynayn		Sanboor	
eye shadow	ماكياج العينين	**faulty**	فيه خلل
makiyaaj		feeh khalal	
al-Aaynayn		**favourite**	مفضل
		mufaddal	
		fax *(noun)*	فاكس
F		faaks	
		February	فبراير
		febraayir	
face	وجه		
wajh			

feel: I feel well	أحس إني	**first class**	الدرجة الأولى
aHiss innee	بخير	ad-daraja	
bi-khayr		al-'oola	
I feel unwell	أحس إني	**first name**	الإسم
aHiss innee	مريض	al-'ism	الشخصي
mareeD		ash-shakhSee	
ferry	قارب	**fish**	سمك
qaarib		samak	
fever	حمى	**fit** (healthy)	بصحة جيدة
Humma		bi-SiHHa jayida	
few: few tourists	سواح قليل	**fizzy**	فوار
suwaaH qaleel		fawwaar	
a few	بعض	**flash**	الفلاش
baAD		al-flaash	
field	حقل	**flat** (noun)	شقة
Haql		shaqqa	
figs	تين	**flat** (adj)	مسطح
teen		musaTTaH	
filling (tooth)	حشو	**flavour**	نكهة
Hashw		nakha	
film	فيلم	**flea**	برغوث
feelm		barghooth	
find	وجد	**flight**	رحلة
wajad,		riHla	
yajid	يجد	**floor** (of room)	أرضية
finger		arDiya	
'oSboA	أصبع	(storey)	طابق
finish (verb)		Taabaq	
khallaS,	خلص	**flower**	زهرة
yekhalleS	يخلص	zahra	
fire		**flu**	إنفلوانزا
naar	نار	enfluanza	
(blaze) Hareeq	حريق	**fly** (insect)	ذبابة
fire extinguisher		zubaaba	
muTfi'at	مطفئة الحريق	**fly** (verb)	طار
al-Hareeq		Taar,	
first	أول	yaTeer	يطير
awwal		**follow**	
first aid	إسعاف أولي	tabaA,	تبع
isAaaf awwalee		yetbaA	يتبع

ENGLISH-ARABIC

English	Arabic
food TaAam	طعام
food poisoning tasammum ghezaa'ee	تسمم غذائي
foot qadam	قدم
on foot maashi	ماشي
football korat al-qadam	كرة القدم
for: for three nights li-thalaathat ayyaam	لثلاثة ايام
who is it for? li-man?	لمن ؟
for you/for me lak/lee	لي / لك
forbidden mamnooA	ممنوع
foreigner ajnabee	أجنبي
forest ghaaba	غابة
forget nasaa, yansaa	نسى ينسى
fork shawka (in road) muftaraq at-Toroq	شوكة مفترق الطرق
form (to fill in) 'istimaara	إستمارة
fortnight usbooAayn	أسبوعين
forward (mail) rasal, yersel	رسل يرسل

English	Arabic
fracture kasr	كسر
free Hurr (of charge) majjaan	حر مجان
French (adj) faransee	فرنسي
French fries baTaaTes maqliyya	بطاطة مقلية
Friday yowm al-jumuAa	يوم الجمعة
fridge thallaaja	ثلاجة
friend Sadeeq	صديق
from min	من
from Cairo to Alexandria min al-qaahira 'ila al-iskandariya	من القاهرة الى الإسكندرية
front (part) muqaddima	مقدمة
in front of amaam	أمام
fruit fawaakeh	فواكه
fry qala, yaqlee	قلى يقلي
full malyaan	مليان
fun: have fun! istamtiA!	إستمتع !
funeral jinaaza	جنازة

85

ENGLISH-ARABIC

funny (*strange*)	غريب	**genuine**	حقيقي
ghareeb		Haqeeqee	
(*amusing*)	مضحك	**get** (*obtain*)	
modHek		HaSal Aala,	حصل على
furniture	أثاث	yeHSel Aala	يحصل على
athaath		**can you tell me**	
further	أبعد	**how to get to ...?**	
abAad		mumkin tiqool	ممكن تقول
fuse	سلك كهربائي	lee keef aSil	لي كيف أصل
silk		li ...?	لـ ... ؟
kahrabaa'ee		**get back** (*return*)	
		rajaA,	رجع
		yerjaA	يرجع
G		**get off**	
		nazal,	نزل
		yanzel	ينزل
		get up	
garage (*for*		qaam,	قام
repairs)	كراج ميكانيكي	yaqoom	يقوم
garaaj		**gin**	دجين
meekaaneeki		djeen	
(*for parking*)	موقف	**girl**	بنت
mowqif	سيارات	bint (*f*)	
sayyaaraat		**girlfriend**	صديقة
garden	حديقة	Sadeeqa	
Hadeeqa		**give**	
garlic	ثوم	ATa,	عطى
thoom		yaATee	يعطي
gas	غاز	**give back**	
ghaaz		rajjaA,	رجع
(*gasoline*)	بنزين	yerajjeA	يرجع
banzeen		**glad**	مسرور
gate	باب	masroor	
baab		**glass** (*for*	
gay	لوطي	*drinking*)	كأس
looTee		ka's	
gear	جير	(*material*)	
geer		zojaaj	زجاج
gents (*toilet*)	طوالیت	**glasses**	نظارات
Twalet	للرجال	naZZaaraat	
li ar-rijaal			

86

English	Arabic
gloves quffaazaat	قفازات
glue gharaa'	غراء
go (away) raaH, yerooH	راح يروح
go away! rooH!	روح !
go down nazal, yanzel	نزل ينزل
go in dakhal, yedkhul	دخل يدخل
go out kharaj, yekhruj	خرج يخرج
go through Aabar, yaAbur	عبر يعبر
go up TalaA, yaTlaA	طلع يطلع
God al-laah	ألله
gold zahab	ذهب
goldsmith zehaibi	ذهبي
good kwayis	كويس
good! Tayyib!	طيب !
goodbye maAa as-salaama	مع السلامة
got: have you got ...? Aindek ...?	عندك ... ؟

English	Arabic
government Hukooma	حكومة
grammar an-naHw	النحو
grandfather jadd	جد
grandmother jadda	جدة
grapefruit graybfroot	كريبفروت
grapes Ainab	عنب
grass Aushb	عشب
grateful mutshakkir	متشكر
greasy mushaHHam	مشحم
green akhdar	أخضر
grey ramaadi	رمادي
grocer's baqqaal	بقال
ground floor at-Taabaq as-suflee	الطابق السفلي
group jamaAa	جماعة
guarantee Damaan	ضمان
guest Dayf	ضيف
guide murshid	مرشد
guidebook kitaab murshid	كتاب مرشد
guitar qeethaara	قيثارة

ENGLISH-ARABIC

English	Arabic
Gulf: the Gulf al-khaleej	الخليج
the Gulf States duwal al-khaleej	دول الخليج
gun (pistol) musaddas	مسدس
(rifle) bunduqiya	بندقية

H

English	Arabic
hair shaAar	شعر
haircut (for men) Hilaaqat ash-shaAar	حلاقة الشعر
(for women) qaS ash-shaAar	قص الشعر
hairdresser Hallaaq	حلاق
half nuSS	نص
half an hour nuSS saAa	نص ساعة
ham laHm al-khinzeer	لحم الخنزير
hammer miTraqa	مطرقة
hand yad	يد
handbag shanTa	شنطة
handkerchief mandeel	منديل
handle (of door etc) meqbaD	مقبض

English	Arabic
hand luggage shanTat al-yad	شنطة اليد
handsome waseem	وسيم
happy saAeed	سعيد
Happy New Year! sana saAeeda!	سنة سعيدة !
harbour meenaa'	ميناء
hard (material) qaasee	قاسي
(difficult) SaAb	صعب
hardware shop Haddaad	حداد
hat qobbaAa	قبعة
hate karah, yakrah	كره، يكره
have (to own) imtalak, yamtalek	امتلك، يمتلك
have you got ...? Aindek ...?	عندك ... ؟
I have to ... laazim ...; (see grammar)	لازم ...
hay fever al-Homma al-qasheya	الحمى القشية
he huwwa (see grammar)	هو
head ra's	رأس
headache sodaA	صداع

88

headlights	النور الأمامي	**this is for her**	هذا لها
an-**noor**		haaza laha;	
al-amaamee		*(see grammar)*	
hear	سمع	**herbs**	أعشاب
sameA,		aAshaab	
yasmaA	يسمع	**here**	هنا
hearing aid	سماعة الأصم	hina	
sammaAat		**hers**	ملكها
al-aSamm		milkhaa	
heart	قلب	**hiccups**	حازوقة
qalb		Haazooqa	
heart attack	نوبة قلبية	**high**	عالي
nowba qalbiya		Aalee	
heat	الحر	**hill**	تل
al-Harr		tell	
heating	تدفئة	**him**	هو
tadfi'a		huwwa	
heavy	ثقيل	**it's him**	هذا هو
thaqeel		haaza huwwa	
heel	كعب	**this is for him**	هذا له
kaAb		haaza lah;	
helicopter	طائرة عمودية	*(see grammar)*	
Taa'ira		**hip**	ورك
Aamoodiya		wark	
hello	أهلا	**hire: for hire**	للإيجار
ahlan		li al-'eejaar	
help *(noun)*	مساعدة	**his**	ـه ..
mosaAada		...-u	
help *(verb)*	ساعد	**his book**	كتابه
saAad,		kitaabu	
yusaAid	يساعد	**it's his**	هذا ملكه
help!	الإغاثة !	haaza milku;	
al-ighaatha!		*(see grammar)*	
her *(object)*	هي	**hit** *(verb)*	ضرب
hiyya		Darab,	
(possessive)	ـها ..	yaDrub	يضرب
...-ha		**hitchhiking**	أطوستوب
her book	كتابها	otostoop	
kitaabha		**hole**	ثقبة
		thuqba	

English	Arabic
holiday	عطلة
AoTla	
(public)	عيد وطني
Aeed waTanee	
home: at home	في البيت
fee al-bayt	
(in my country)	في بلدي
fee baladee	
go home	يروح للبيت
yarooH li al-bayt	
honey	عسل
Aasal	
hope (verb)	
itmannaa,	اتمنى
yatamannaa	يتمنى
horrible	مفزع
mufziA	
horse	حصان
HiSaan	
hospital	مستشفى
mustashfa	
hospitality	ضيافة
Diyaafa	
hot	حار
Haarr	
(to taste)	حريف
Hirreef	
hotel (de luxe)	فندق
funduq	
(small)	نزل
nazl	
hour	ساعة
saAa	
house	منزل
manzil	
how?	كيف ؟
kayf?	
how are you?	كيف حالك ؟
kayf Haalek?	

English	Arabic
how are things?	كيف الأمور ؟
kayf al-'umoor?	
how many/	
much?	كم ؟
kam?	
humid	رطب
ruTb	
hungry: I'm	
hungry	أنا جوعان
ana jawAan	
hurry: hurry up!	بسرعة ا
bi-surAa!	
hurt: it hurts	يوجع
yoojaA	
husband	زوج
zowj	

I

I	أنا
ana;	
(see grammar)	
ice	ثلج
thalj	
ice cream	أيس كريم
ays kreem	
idiot	بليد
baleed	
if	إذا
iza	
ignition	جهاز الإشعال
jihaaz al-ishAal	
ill	مريض
mareeD	
immediately	فوراً
fowran	
important	مهم
muhimm	

ENGLISH-ARABIC

impossible mustaHeel	مستحيل
in: in London fee london	في لندن
in England fee inglaterra	في إنجلترا
in English bi al-ingleeziya	بالإنجليزية
is he in? huwwa mowjood?	هو موجود ؟
included: ... included fee ...	في ...
indigestion maghaS	مغص
industry SinaAa	صناعة
infection Aadwa	عدوى
information maAloomat	معلومات
information bureau 'istiAlaamaat	إستعلامات
injection Hoqna	حقنة
injured moSaab bi jurooH	مصاب بجروح
inner tube unboob daakhilee	أنبوب داخلي
innocent baree'	بريء
insect Hashara	حشرة
insect repellent Taarid li al-Hasharaat	طارد للحشرات

insurance ta'meen	تأمين
intelligent shaaTir	شاطر
interesting shayeq	شيق
invitation daAwa	دعوة
invoice faatoora	فاتورة
Iran eeraan (f)	إيران
Iraq al-Airaaq (f)	العراق
Ireland irlanda	إرلندا
iron (metal) Hadeed	حديد
(for clothes) makwaa	مكواة
Islam islaam	إسلام
island jazeera	جزيرة
Israel israa'eel (f)	إسرائيل
it huwwa (m) hiyya (f); (see grammar)	هو هي

J

jack (car) raafiAa	رافعة
jacket jaakeet	جاكيت

91

ENGLISH-ARABIC

jam
merabba مربى

January
yanaayer يناير

jaw
fakk فك

jazz
mooseeqa djaaz موسيقى جاز

jeans
jeenz جينز

jeweller's
taajir تاجر
mojowharaat مجوهرات

jewellery
mojowharaat مجوهرات

job
waZeefa وظيفة

joke
nokta نكتة

Jordan
al-ordon (f) الاردن

journey
riHla رحلة

jug
ibreeq إبريق

juice
AaSeer عصير

July
yooliyu يوليو

junction (road) ملتقى الطرق
multaqa at-
Toroq

June
yooniyu يونيو

just
bass بس

just two
ithnayn bass إثنين بس

K

key
miftaaH مفتاح

kidneys
kolya كلية

kill
qatal, قتل
yaqtul يقتل

kilo
keelo كيلو

kilometre
keelomeeter كيلوميتر

kind (adj)
Tayyib طيب

kiss (noun)
boosa بوسة

kiss (verb)
baas, باس
yeboos يبوس

kitchen
maTbakh مطبخ

knee
rokba ركبة

knife
sikkeen سكين

know
Araf, عرف
yaArif يعرف

I don't know
maa aArif ما أعرف

Koran
al-qur'aan القرآن

Kuwait
al-kuwayt (f) الكويت

L

ladder	سلم	sullam
ladies (room)	طواليت للسيدات	twalet li as-sayidaat
lady	سيدة	sayyida
lake	بحيرة	boHayra
lamb	خروف	kharoof
lamp	لمبا	lamba
language	لغة	lugha
large	كبير	kabeer
last	أخير	akheer
last year	العام الماضي	al-Aam al-maaDi
late	متأخر	met'akhir
laugh	ضحك يضحك	DaHak, yaDHak
laundry	ملابس للغسل	malaabis li al-ghasl
(place)	مغسل الملابس	maghsal al-malaabis
law	القانون	al-qaanoon

lawsuit	دعوى	daAwa
lawyer	محامي	muHaamee
laxative	مسهل	mus-hil
lazy	كسلان	kaslaan
leaflet	كراسة	kurraasa
leak	تسرب	tasarrub
learn	تعلم يتعلم	taAallam, yataAallam
leather	جلد	jild
leave (behind)	ترك يترك	tarak, yatruk
(go away)	راح يروح	raaH, yerooH
(forget)	نسى ينسى	nasaa, yansa
Lebanon	لبنان	lubnaan (f)
left	يسار	yasaar
on the left (of)	على اليسار	Aala al-yasaar
left-handed	أعسر	aAsar
left luggage	خزانة للشنط	khizaana li ash-shonooT
leg	رجل	rijl

ENGLISH-ARABIC

lemon	ليمون	**light bulb**	مبا
laymoon		lamba	
lemonade	ليمونادة	**lighter**	داحة
limonaada		qaddaaHa	
lens (camera)	عدسة	**like** (verb)	
Aadasa		aHibb,	حب
less	أقل	yaHibb	حب
'aqall		**I would like ...**	
lesson	درس	ureed ...	ريد ...
dars		**like** (as)	ي
letter (in mail)	خطاب	zayy	
khiTaab		**lip**	فاه
letterbox	صندوق البريد	shafaah	
Sundooq		**lipstick**	وج
al-bareed		rooj	
library	مكتبة	**listen (to)**	
maktaba		istamiA,	ستمع
Libya	ليبيا	yastamiA	ستمع
leebiyaa		**litre**	يترو
licence	رخصة	leetru	
rokhSa		**little**	غير
lid	غطاء	Sagheer	
ghaTaa'		**a little bit (of)**	وية
lie down		shwayya	
irtaaH,	ارتاح	**live** (in town etc)	
yartaaH	يرتاح	sakan,	كن
life	حياة	yaskun	سكن
Hayaa		**liver**	بد
lift (elevator)	مصعد	kabid	
misAad		**living room**	رفة الجلوس
light (in room etc)	النور	ghurfat al-juloos	
an-noor		**lock** (noun)	فل
(on car)	المصابيح	qafl	
al-maSaabeeH		**lock** (verb)	
have you got a		qafal,	فل
light?	عندك	yaqfal	فل
Aindek kabreet?	كبريت ؟	**long**	ويل
light (not heavy)	خفيف	Taweel	
khafeef		**a long time**	دة طويلة
		mudda Taweela	

94

English	Arabic	English	Arabic
look at	شاف	good luck!	حظ سعيد !
shaaf,	يشوف	HaZZ saAeed!	
yashoof		luggage	حقائب
look like	أشبه	Haqaa'ib	
ashbah,	يشبه	lunch	غداء
yushbih		ghadaa'	
look for	دور على	lungs	رئتين
dawwar Aala,	يدور على	ri'atayn	
yudawwir Aala			
look out!	خذ بالك !		
khus baalek!			

M

English	Arabic	English	Arabic
sorry	شاحنة		
shaaHina			
lose	ضيع	mad	أحمق
DayyaA,	يضيع	aHmaq	
yuDayyiA		magazine	مجلة
lost property		majalla	
office	مكتب	mail	البريد
maktab	المفقودات	al-bareed	
al-mafqoodaat		make	
lot: a lot	كثير	sawwa,	سوى
katheer		yesawwee	يسوي
a lot of ...	كثير من ...	make-up	ماكياج
katheer min ...		makiyaaj	
a lot warmer	ادفئ بكثير	man	رجل
adfa' bi-katheer		rajul	
loud	صوت عالي	manager	مدير
Sowt Aali		mudeer	
love (noun)	الحب	many	كثير
al-Hubb		katheer	
love (verb)	أحب	many ...	كثير من ...
aHibb,	يحب	katheer min ...	
yuHibb		map	خريطة
lovely	هائل	khareeTa	
haa'il		March	مارس
low	منخفض	maares	
munkhafiD		market	سوق
luck	حظ	sooq	
HaZZ		married	متزوج
		mutzawwij	

English	Arabic
mascara	مسكارا
maskaara	
match (light)	كبريت
kebreet	
(sport)	مباراة
mubaaraa	
material (cloth)	قماش
qomaash	
matter: it doesn't	
matter	ما عليش
maA-leesh	
mattress	مرتبة
martaba	
Mauritania	موريطانيا
mooreeTaaniya	
May	مايو
maayoo	
maybe	ممكن
mumkin	
me	انا
ana	
me too	انا كمان
ana kamaan;	
(see grammar)	
meal	وجبة
wajba	
measles	حصبة
HaSba	
meat	لحم
laHm	
Mecca	مكة
makka	
medicine	دواء
dawaa'	
meeting	إجتماع
'ijtimaA	
melon	شمام
shamaam	

English	Arabic
mend	صلح
SallaH,	يصلح
yeSalliH	
men's room (US)	طوالیت
twalet li ar-rijaal	للرجال
menu	
qaa'imat	قائمة الأطعمة
al-'atAima	
message	رسالة
resaala	
metal	معدن
maAden	
metre	ميتر
meeter	
middle	وسط
wasaT	
Middle East	الشرق الاوسط
ash-sharq	
al-'awsaT	
milk	حليب
Haleeb	
minaret	مأذنة
mi'zana	
mine: it's mine	هذا ملكي
haaza milkee	
mineral water	مياه معدنية
miyaah	
maAdiniya	
minute	دقيقة
daqeeqa	
mirror	مراية
meraaya	
Miss	انسة
aanisa; (see	
Things Arabic)	
miss (train etc)	
faat,	فات
yafoot	يفوت

96

ENGLISH-ARABIC

he missed the
train القطار فاته
al-QiTaar faatu
I miss you وحشتيني
waHashteeni
mistake غلطة
ghalTa
modern عصري
AaSree
monastery دير
dayr
Monday يوم الإثنين
yowm al-ithnayn
money فلوس
fuloos
month شهر
shahr
moon قمر
qamar
more أكثر
akthar
no more ... خلص ...
... khallaS
I've no more ... خلص ...
... khallaS
no more coffee, يكفي من
thanks قهوة ، شكرا
yakfee min
qahwa, shukran
morning صباح
SabaaH
Morocco المغرب
al-maghreb (f)
mosaic فسيفساء
fusayfisaa'
Moslem
(adj)
muslim مسلم
mosque مسجد
masjid

mosquito ناموس
naamoos
mosquito net ناموسية
naamoosiya
most (of) أغلب
'aghlab
mother أم
umm (f)
motorbike دراجة نارية
darraaja naariya
motorway طريق رئيسي
Tareeq ra'eesee
mountain جبل
jabal
mouse فار
fa'r
moustache شارب
shaareb
mouth فم
fam
movie فيلم
feelm
movie theater
(US) سينما
seenima
Mr السيد
as-sayid; (see
Things Arabic)
Mrs السيدة
as-sayida; (see
Things Arabic)
much كثير
katheer
muezzin مأذن
mu'azzin
muscle عضلة
AaDala
museum متحف
matHaf

97

English	Arabic	English	Arabic
mushrooms fotr	فطر	**nappy** HaffaaZa	حفاظة
music mooseeqa	موسيقى	**narrow** Dayyiq	ضيق
must: I/she must laazim	لازم	**nationality** jinsiya	جنسية
my ...-ee	... ي	**natural** TabeeAee	طبيعي
my book kitaabee; (see grammar)	كتابي	**near** qareeb min	قريب من
		the nearest ... 'aqrab ...	أقرب ...

N		**nearly** taqreeban	تقريبا
		necessary Darooree	ضروري
nail (in wall) mismaar	مسمار	**neck** Aunuq	عنق
nailfile mibrad aZaafeer	مبرد أظافير	**necklace** Auqd	عقد
nail polish molammiA li al-aZaafeer	ملمع للأظافير	**need: I need ...** aHtaaj...	أحتاج ...
		needle 'ibra	إبرة
nail polish remover muzeel molammiA al-aZaafeer	مزيل ملمع الأظافير	**negative** (film) Sura Salbiya	صورة صلبية
		nervous qaliq	قلق
naked Aari	عار	**never** abadan	أبدا
name ism	إسم	**new** jadeed	جديد
what's your name? eesh ismek?	إيش إسمك ؟	**news** akhbaar	أخبار
my name is Jim ismee 'Jim'	إسمي جيم	**newspaper** jareeda	جريدة
napkin mandeel al-maa'ida	منديل المائدة	**New Year** al-Aam al-jadeed	العام الجديد

next	القادم	**north**	شمال
al-qaadim		shamaal	
(following)	الجاي	**nose**	أنف
al-jaay		anf	
next to	بجانب	**not**	مو
bi-jaanib		moo;	
nice *(person)*	لطيف	*(see grammar)*	
laTeef		**notebook**	دفتر
(place)	جميل	daftar	
jameel		**nothing**	لا شيء
(food)	كويس	laa shay'	
kwayis		**November**	نوفمبر
night	ليل	noovember	
layl		**now**	الآن
nightdress	قميص النوم	al-aan	
qameeS		**number**	نمرة
an-nowm		nemra	
Nile: the Nile	النيل	*(house, phone)*	رقم
an-neel *(f)*		raqm	
no	لا	**nurse**	ممرضة
laa		mumarriDa	
no ...	ممنوع ...		
mamnooA ...			
there is no ...	ما في ...		
maa fee ...			
I've no ...	ما عندي ...		
maa Aindee ...;			

O

(see grammar)		**October**	أكتوبر
nobody	لا أحد	oktoober	
laa aHad		**office**	مكتب
noise	ضجة	maktab	
Dajja		**often**	غالباً
noisy	كثير الضجة	ghaaliban	
katheer ad-Dajja		**oil**	زيت
non-smoking	مكان ممنوع	zayt	
makaan		**OK**	طيب
mamnooA feeh	فيه التدخين	Tayyib	
at-tadkheen		**I'm OK**	طيب
normal	عادي	Tayyib	
Aadi			

99

ENGLISH-ARABIC

old *(not new)*	قديم	**optician**	نظاراتي
qadeem		naZaaraatee	
(not young)	عجوز	**or**	أو
Aajooz		ow	
how old are you?	كم عمرك ؟	**orange** *(fruit)*	برتقال
kam Aumrek?		burtoqaal	
I'm 25 years old	عمري خمسة	**orange** *(colour)*	برتقالي
Aumree khamsa wa Aishreen sana	و عشرين سنة	burtoqaalee	
		orchestra	الأوركسترا
		al-oorkestraa	
omelette	أومليت	**other**	
oomleet		aakhar *(m)*	آخر
Oman	عمان	ukhraa *(f)*	أخرى
Aommaan *(f)*		**our**	..نا
on *(on top of)*	فوق	...-naa	
fowq		**our car**	سيارتنا
(upon)	على	sayyaaratnaa;	
Aala		*(see grammar)*	
on the floor	على الأرض	**ours**	ملكنا
Aalal-'arD		milknaa	
one *(number)*		**out: she's out**	هي مو
waaHid *(m)*	واحد	hiyya moo	موجودة
waaHida *(f)*	واحدة	mowjooda	
onion	بصل	**outside**	برة
baSal		barra	
only	بس	**over** *(above)*	فوق
bass		fowq	
open *(adj)*	مفتوح	*(finished)*	خلص
maftooH		khallaS	
open *(verb)*		**over there**	هناك
fataH,	فتح	hinaak	
yeftaH	يفتح	**oyster**	محار
opera	أوبيري	maHaar	
opeeraa			
operation	عملية	# P	
Aamaliya			
opposite: opposite the ...	أمام ...	**package**	الطرد
amaam ...		Tard	

100

ENGLISH-ARABIC

English	Arabic
packet (of cigarettes etc) Aulba	علبة
page SafHa	صفحة
pain alam	ألم
painful mu'lim	مؤلم
painkiller musakkin li al-alam	مسكن للألم
painting Soora	صورة
palace qaSr	قصر
Palestine falasTeen (f)	فلسطين
panties kalsoon	كلسون
paper waraq	ورق
parcel Tard	طرد
pardon? Aafwan?	عفوًا ؟
parents waalidayn	والدين
park (noun) Hadeeqa	حديقة
park (verb) waqqaf, yowqif	وقف يوقف
parking lot (US) maHaTTat sayyaaraat	محطة سيارات
part (noun) juz'	جزء

English	Arabic
party (celebration) Hafla	حفلة
(group) majmooAa	مجموعة
pass (mountain) maDyaq	مضيق
passport jawaaz safar	جواز سفر
path Tareeq	طريق
pavement raSeef	رصيف
pay dafaA, yadfaA	دفع يدفع
peach khookh	خوخ
peanuts fool soodaanee	فول سوداني
pear komethra	كوميثرا
peas bazilla	البازيلا
pedal dawwaasa	دواسة
pedestrian crossing khaTT al-mushaah	خط المشاه
pen qalam Hibr	قلم حبر
pencil qalam raSaaS	قلم رصاص
penicillin penisileen	بنيسلين
penknife sikkeen al-jayb	سكين الجيب
people naas	ناس

101

pepper *(spice)*   فلفل
felfel
  red pepper   فلفل أحمر
felfel aHmar
per cent   في المئة
fee al-mi'a
perfect   تمام
tamaam
perfume   عطر
AeTr
period *(woman's)*   العادة
al-Aada
person   شخص
shakhS
petrol   بنزين
banzeen
petrol station   محطة بنزين
maHaTTat
banzeen
phone *(verb)*
'ettaSal bi   اتصل بالتلفون
at-tilifoon,
yattaSil bi   يتصل بالتلفون
at-tilifoon
phone box   تلفون عمومي
tilifoon
Aumoomee
phone number   رقم التلفون
raqm at-tilifoon
photograph *(noun)*   صورة
Soora
photograph *(verb)*
Sawwar,   صور
yeSawwir   يصور
phrase book   كتاب تعبيرات
kitaab
taAeeraat
pickpocket   نشال
nashaal

piece   قطعة
qeTAa
pilgrimage   الحج
al-Hajj
pill *(contraceptive)*   حبوب منع
Hoboob manA
al-Haml   الحمل
pillow   وسادة
wisaada
pin   دبوس
daboos
pineapple   أناناس
ananaas
pink   وردي
wardee
pipe   أنبوب
anboob
(to smoke)   بيبة
beeba
(Arabic type)   غليون
ghalyoon
pity: it's a pity   خسارة
khasaara
plane   طائرة
Taa'ira
plant   نبات
nabaat
plastic   بلاستيك
blaasteek
plastic bag   كيس من
kees min
al-blaasteek   البلاستيك
plate   صحن
SaHn
play *(theatre)*   مسرحية
masraHiya
play *(verb)*
laAeb,   لعب
yalAab

ENGLISH-ARABIC

English	Arabic	English	Arabic
pleasant laTeef	لطيف	**post** *(verb)* rasal, yarsel	رسل يرسل
please min faDlek	من فضلك	**postcard** biTaaqa bareediya	بطاقة بريدية
pleased masroor	مسرور	**poster** *(for room)* Soora	صورة
pliers kammaasha	كماشة	*(in street)* eAlaan	إعلان
plug *(electric)* qaabis	قابس	**post office** maktab al-bareed	مكتب البريد
(in sink) saddaada	سدادة	**potato** baTaaTes	بطاطس
plum barkuk	برقوق	**pound** *(money)* junayh	جنيه
pocket jayb	جيب	**prawn** jambaree	جمبري
poison summ	سم	**prayer** Salaah	صلاة
police shorTa, boolees	شرطة بوليس	**prayer mat** sajjaadat as-Salaah	سجادة الصلاة
policeman shorTee	شرطي	**pregnant** Haamil	حامل
police station markaz ash-shorTa	مركز الشرطة	**prescription** waSfa Tibbiya	وصفة طبية
polite mu'addab	مؤدب	**present** *(gift)* hadiyya	هدية
politics as-siyaasa	السياسة	**pretty** Zareef	ظريف
polluted mulawwath	ملوث	**price** siAr	سعر
poor faqeer	فقير	**priest** qasees	قسيس
pop music mooseeqa Aasriya	موسيقى عصرية	**prison** sijn	سجن
pork laHm al-khinzeer	لحم الخنزير	**private** khaaS	خاص
possible mumkin	ممكن		

ENGLISH-ARABIC

problem mushkila	مشكلة	**quick** sareeA	سريع
prohibited mamnooA	ممنوع	**quickly** bi-surAa	بسرعة
pronounce naTaq, yanToq	نطق ينطق	**quiet** haadi'	هادئ
pull saHab, yasHab	سحب يسحب	**quite** (*fairly*) shwaya	شوية
pump boomba	بومبة		

R

English	Arabic	English	Arabic
puncture thaqb	ثقب	**rabbit** 'arnab	أرنب
purple urjuwaanee	أرجواني	**radio** raadiyo	رايدو
purse kees	كيس	**railway** as-sekka al-Hadeediya	السكة الحديدية
push dafaA, yadfaA	دفع يدفع	**rain** al-maTar	المطر
put HaTT, yeHuTT	حط يحط	**it's raining** yamTur	يمطر
pyjamas beejaama	بيجاما	**raincoat** meEATaf	معطف
pyramids al-ahraam	الأهرام	**Ramadan** ramaDaan	رمضان
		rape 'ightiSaab	إغتصاب

Q

English	Arabic	English	Arabic
		raspberry toot shookee	توت شوكي
		rat jirz	جرز
Qatar qaTar (*f*)	قطر	**raw** ghair maTbookh	غير مطبوخ
question su'aal	سؤال	**razor** moos al-Hilaaqa	موس الحلاقة
queue Saff	صف	**razor blade** shafra	شفرة

104

English	Arabic
read	قرأ
qara',	
yaqra'	يقرأ
ready (person)	مستعد
mustaAidd	
(thing)	جاهز
jaahiz	
rear lights	أضواء خلفية
aDwaa' khalfiya	
receipt	ايصال
'eeSaal	
record (music)	أسطوانة
'osTowaana	
record player	جهاز تشغيل
jihaaz tashgheel	الأسطوانة
al-'ostowaana	
red	أحمر
aHmar	
Red Sea	البحر الأحمر
al-baHr	
al-aHmar	
religion	ديانة
diyaana	
remember: I	
remember	اتذكر
atazakkar	
rent (verb)	استأجر
ista'jar,	
yasta'jir	يستأجر
repair	صلح
SallaH,	
yeSalliH	يصلح
repeat	اعاد
eAad,	
yeAeed	يعيد
reservation	حجز
Hajz	
rest (remainder)	الباقي
al-baaqee	

English	Arabic
(sleep)	إستراحة
esteraaHa	
restaurant	مطعم
maTAam	
restroom (US)	طوإليت
Twalet	
reverse (gear)	غيار السير
ghiyaar as-sayr	الى الوراء
ila al-wara	
reverse charge	تحويل تكلفة
call	التلفون
taHweel taklifat	
at-tilifoon	
rheumatism	مرض
maraD	الروماتيزم
ar-rumateezm	
rib	ضلع
DilA	
rich	غني
ghanee	
right (correct)	صحيح
SaHeeH	
(side)	يمين
yameen	
on the right (of)	على اليمين
Aala al-yameen	
ring (on finger)	خاتم
khaatam	
river	نهر
nahr	
Riyal	ريال
riyaal	
road	طريق
Tareeq	
(in town)	شارع
shaariA	
roll	خبز
khobz	
roof	سقف
saqf	

room	غرفة	**safety pin**	دبوس
ghurfa		daboos	
rope	حبل	**salad**	سلاطة
Habl		salaata	
rose	وردة	**salt**	ملح
warda		melH	
route	طريق	**same**	نفس
Tareeq		nafs	
rubber	مطاط	**sandals**	جزمة
maTTaaT		jazma	
(eraser)		**sandwich**	سندويتش
mimHaah	ممحاه	sandweetsh	
rubber band	لاستيك	**sanitary towel**	حفاظة نسائية
laasteek		HaffaaZa	
rubbish *(refuse)*	زبالة	nisaa'iya	
zebaala		**Saturday**	يوم السبت
rucksack	جربندية	yowm as-sabt	
jarabandiya		**sauce**	صلصة
rude	قليل الأدب	SalSa	
qaleel al-'adab		**Saudi Arabia**	السعودية
rug	سجادة	as-saAoodiya	
sajjaada		**sausage**	سوسيس
ruins	أنقاض	soosees	
anqaaD		**say**	قال،
rum	روم	qaal,	يقول
room		yeqool	
run	جرى	**scarf** *(neck)*	وشاح
jara,		wishaaH	
yajree	يجرى	**school**	مدرسة
		madrasa	
		scissors	مقص
S		maqaSS	
		screwdriver	مفك
sad	حزين	mafakk	
Hazeen		**sea**	بحر
safe *(thing)*	مأمون	baHr	
ma'moon		**seaside: at the**	
(person)		**seaside**	على شاطئ
saleem	سليم	Aala shaaTi'	البحر
		al-baHr	

ENGLISH-ARABIC

seat	مقعد
maqAad	
seat belt	حزام السلامة
Hizaam	
as-salaama	
second (*in time*)	ثانية
thaaniya	
see	
shaaf,	شاف
yashoof	يشوف
I can't see it	مو أشوفه
moo ashoofhu	
see you	
tomorrow	سأشوفك بكرة
sa-ashoofek	
bukra	
I see	
(*understand*)	
afham	أفهم
sell	
baA,	باع
yabeeA	يبيع
sellotape(R)	سيلوتيب
seeloteep	
send	
rasal,	رسل
yarsel	يرسل
separate	منفصل
monfaSel	
September	سبتمبر
seeptember	
serviette	منديل المائدة
mandeel	
al-maa'ida	
several	عدة
Aiddat	
sew	
khayaT,	خيط
yekhayeT	يخيط

shade: in the	
shade	في الظل
fee ad-Dill	
shampoo	شامبو
shamboo	
share (*verb*)	قسم
qasam,	يقسم
yaqsim	
shaving brush	فرشة حلاقة
forshit Hila'a	
shaving foam	صابون الحلاقة
Saaboon	
al-Hilaaqa	
she	هي
hiyya;	
(*see grammar*)	
sheet	شرشف
sharshaf	
sheik	شيخ
shaykh	
ship	سفينة
safeena	
shirt	قميص
qameeS	
shoe laces	رباط الحذاء
ribaaT al-Hizaa'	
shoe polish	ملمع الأحذية
molammiA	
al-aHziya	
shoe repairer	خراز
kharraaz	
shoes	أحذية
aHziya	
shop	دكان
dukkaan	
shopping:	
go shopping	يتسوق
yatsawaq	
short	قصير
qaSSeer	

107

ENGLISH-ARABIC

shorts بنطلون شورت
bantaloon shoort

shoulder كتف
ketf

shower (wash) دوش
doosh

shy خجول
khajool

sick مريض
mareeD

signature توقيع
towqeeA

silk حرير
Hareer

silver فضة
feDDa

similar متشابه
mutashaabih

simple بسيط
baseeT

since (time) منذ
munzu

sing
ghanna, غنى
yughannee يغني

single (unmarried) أعزب
aAzab

sister أخت
ukht (f)

sit down
jalas, جلس
yajles يجلس

size مقاس
maqaas

skin بشرة
bashara

skinny نحيف
naHeef

skirt تنورة
tannoora

sky سماء
samaa'

sleep
naam, نام
yenaam ينام

sleeper (train) عربة نوم
Aarabat nowm

sleeping bag كيس لنوم
kees li-noom

sleeping pill حبوب منومة
Huboob
munawwima

slide (photo) سلايد
'slide'

slim نحيف
naHeef

slippers شبشب
shebsheb

slow بطيء
baTee'

slowly ببطء
bi-boT'

small صغير
Sagheer

smell (verb)
shamm, شم
yashumm يشم

smile (verb)
ibtasam, ابتسم
yabtasim يبتسم

smoke (noun) دخان
dokhaan

smoke (verb)
dakhan, دخن
yudakhin يدخن

snake حية
Haya

so: so slow بطيء جداً
baTee' jiddan

soap صابون
Saaboon

socket مقبس
maqbas كهربائي
kahrabaa'ee

socks جوارب
jawaarib

soft ناعم
naAim

soft drink مشروبات
mashroobaat بدون كحول
bidoon koHool

sole (of shoe) نعل
naAl

Somalia صوماليا
Soomaaliya

some (pronoun) بعض
baAD

some water بعض المياه
baAD al-mayah

somebody شخص ما
shakhS maa

something شيء ما
shay' maa

sometimes أحيانا
aHyaanan

son إبن
ibn

song أغنية
ughniya

soon قريب
qareeb

sore ألم
alam

**I've got a sore
throat** عندي ألم في
Aindee alam fee الحلق
al-Halq

sorry آسف
aasif

I'm sorry انا آسف
ana aasif

so-so متوسط
mutwasseT

soup شربة
shorba

sour مر
murr

south جنوب
janoob

spanner مفتاح صواميل
miftaaH
Sawaameel

spare parts قطع غيار
qetaA ghiyaar

spark plug البوجية
al-boojiya

speak تكلم،
takallam, يتكلم
yetkallam

do you speak ...? تتكلم ... ؟
titkallam ...?

speed limit حد السرعة
Hadd as-surAa

spider عنكبوت
Aankaboot

spoke قضيب الدراجة
qaDeeb
ad-darraaja

spoon ملعقة
melAaqa

sport رياضة
riyaaDa

spring (season) فصل الربيع
faSl ar-rabeeA

square (in town) ميدان
maydaan

stadium ستاض
sTaad

ENGLISH-ARABIC

stairs	سلم
sullam	
stamp	طابع
TaabaA	
star	نجمة
najma	
station	محطة
maHaTTa	
stay (verb: in hotel etc)	
nazal,	نزل
yanzel	ينزل
steak	بفتيك
bifteek	
steal	
saraq,	سرق
yasreq	يسرق
steep (hill)	شديد
shadeed	
al-inHidaar	الإنحدار
steering wheel	عجلة القيادة
Aajalat	
al-qiyaada	
still (adverb)	لسة
lissa	
stockings	جوارب نسائية
jawaarib	
nisaa'iya	
stomach	معدة
maAida	
stomach ache	ألم في المعدة
alam fee	
al-maAida	
stone	حجرة
Hajara	
stop (bus etc)	موقف
mowqif	
stop (verb)	وقف
waqaf,	يقف
yaqif	

storm	عاصفة
AaSifa	
story	حكاية
Hikaaya	
straight: straight ahead	على طول
Aala Tool	
strange (odd)	غريب
ghareeb	
strawberry	فراولة
faraawla	
stream	جدول
jadwal	
street	شارع
shaariA	
string	دبارة
dubaara	
stroke (attack)	نوبة
nawba	
strong (person)	قوي
qawee	
(material)	متين
mateen	
student	
Taalib (m)	طالب
Taaliba (f)	طالبة
stupid	غبي
ghabee	
suburbs	ضواحي
DawaaHee	
Sudan	السودان
as-soodaan (f)	
suddenly	فجأة
faj'a	
Suez Canal	قناة السويز
qanaat	
as-suweez (f)	
sugar	سكر
sukkar	

110

ENGLISH-ARABIC

suit	بدلة
badla	
suitcase	شنطة
shanTa	
summer	فصل الصيف
faSl as-Sayf	
sun	شمس
shams	
sunburn	حرقة الشمس
Harqat ash-shams	
Sunday	يوم الأحد
yowm al-aHad	
sunglasses	نظارات شمس
naZZaaraat shams	
sunstroke	ضربة الشمس
Darbat ash-shams	
suntan lotion	محلول ضد الشمس
maHlool Didd ash-shams	
supermarket	سوبرماركت
soobermaarkeet	
surname	اللقب
al-laqab	
sweater	جرزي
jerzee	
sweet (noun)	حلوى
Halwa	
sweet (adj)	حلو
Hilw	
swim	سبح
sabaH,	
yasbaH	يسبح
swimming costume	مايو السباحة
maayoo as-sibaaHa	
swimming pool	مسبح
masbaH	

swimming trunks	شورط السباحة
shoort as-sibaaHa	
switch (electric)	مفتاح
miftaaH	
Syria	سوريا
sooriya	

T

table	طاولة
Taawila	
table tennis	كرة الطاولة
korat at-Taawila	
take	أخذ
akhaz,	
ya'khuz	ياخذ
take away (remove)	نزع
nazaA,	
yanzaA	ينزع
talk	تحدث
taHaddath,	
yataHaddath	يتحدث
tall	طويل
Taweel	
tap	صنبور
Sanboor	
tape (cassette)	شريط
shareeT	
taste	ذوق
zowq	
taxi	تاكسي
taaksee	
tea	شاي
shaay	
teach	درس
darras,	
yudarris	يدرس

111

teacher muAallim	معلم	**theatre** masraH	مسرح
team fareeq	فريق	**their** ...-hum	..هم
teapot 'ibreeq shaay	إبريق شاي	**their book** kitaabhum; (see grammar)	كتابهم
telegram barqiya	برقية		
telephone (noun)		**theirs** milkhum	ملكهم
tilifoon, al-haatif	تلفون الهاتف	**them** hum; (see grammar)	هم
television tilivisiyoon	تلفزيون	**then** daak al-waqt	داك الوقت
tennis tinees	تنيس	**there** hinaak	هناك
tent khayma	خيمة	**there is/are ...** feeh ...	فيه ...
terrible mofzeA	مفزع	**is/are there ...?** feeh ...?	فيه ... ؟
terrific raa'iA	رائع	**there isn't/aren't ...** maa feeh ...	ما فيه ...
than min	من		
uglier than aqbaH min; (see grammar)	أقبح من	**thermometer** miqiyaas al-Haraara	مقياس الحرارة
thank shakar, yashkur	شكر يشكر	**thermos flask** termoos	ترموس
thank you shukran	شكراً	**these** (adj) dool (pronoun) haa-dool	دول هادول
that (one) zaalek (m) tilka (f); (see grammar)	ذلك تلك	**they** hum; (see grammar)	هم
the al-...	الـ	**thick** sameek	سميك
the book al-kitaab; (see grammar)	الكتاب	**thief** leSS	لص

ENGLISH-ARABIC

thigh	فخض	**ticket**	تذكرة
fakhD		tazkira	
thin	رقيق	**tie** (*necktie*)	كرباطة
raqeeq		krabaaTa	
thing	شيء	**tight**	ضيق
shay'		Dayeq	
think	فكر	**tights**	جوارب نسائية
fakkar,		jawaareb	
yefakkir	يفكر	nisaa'iya	
thirsty: I'm		**time**	مدة
thirsty	أنا عطشان	mudda	
ana AaTshaan		**on time**	في الوقت المحدد
this (one)		fee al-waqt	
haaza (m)	هذا	al-muHaddad	
haazi (f)	هذه	**what time is it?**	الساعة كم ؟
those (*adj*)		as-saAa kam?	
dool	دول	**timetable**	جدول
(pronoun)		jadwal	
haa-dool	هادول	**tin-opener**	فتاحة العلب
thread	خيط	fattaaHat	
khayT		al-Aulab	
throat	حلق	**tip**	بقشيش
Halq		baqsheesh	
through	عبر	**tire** (*US*)	إطار
Aabr		'iTaar	
throw	رمى	**tired**	تعبان
ramaa,		taAbaan	
yarmee	يرمي	**tissues**	كلينكس
throw away	طرح في الزبالة	kleeneks	
TaraH fee		**to: I'm going to**	
az-zabaal		**Cairo**	أنا أروح الى القاهرة
yaTraH fee	يطرح في الزبالة	ana arooH	
az-zabaala		ilal-qahira	
thunderstorm	عاصفة	**I'm going to the**	
AaSifa		**station**	أنا أروح الى المحطة
Thursday	يوم الخميس	ana arooH	
yowm		ilal-maHaTTa	
al-khamees		**tobacco**	دخان
		dukhaan	

today	اليوم	**toothpaste**	معجون
al-yowm		maAjoon	الأسنان
toe	أصبع القدم	al-asnaan	
oSboA al-qadam		**torch**	مصباح يدوي
together	معاً	mesbaaH	
maAan		yadawee	
toilet	طواليت	**tourist**	سائح
Twalet		saa'iH	
toilet paper	ورق الطواليت	**towel**	فوطة
waraq Twalet		fooTa	
tomato	طماطم	**town**	مدينة
TamaaTem		madeena	
tomorrow	بكرى	**traditional**	تقليدي
bukra		taqleedee	
the day after		**traffic**	حركة المرور
tomorrow	بعد بكرى	Harakat	
baAd bukra		al-moroor	
tongue	لسان	**traffic jam**	ازدحام
lisaan		izdiHaam	المرور
tonight	الليلة	al-moroor	
al-layla		**traffic lights**	اشارات
tonsillitis	التهاب اللواز	'ishaaraat	المرور
iltihaab		al-moroor	
al-luwaaz		**train**	قطار
too (also)	كمان	qiTaar	
kamaan		**trainers**	تراينرز
(too small etc)	جداً	'trainers'	
jiddan		**translate**	
too big	كبير جداً	tarjam,	ترجم
kabeer jiddan		yutarjim	يترجم
too much	كثير جداً	**travel agent's**	
katheer jiddan		wikaalat	وكالة سفريات
not too much	مو كثير	safariyaat	
moo katheer		**traveller's cheque**	شيك سياحي
tooth	سن	sheek siyaaHee	
sinn		**tree**	شجرة
toothache	وجع أسنان	shajara	
wajaA asnaan		**tremendous**	هائل
toothbrush	فرشة أسنان	haa'il	
forshat asnaan			

ENGLISH-ARABIC

trip *(journey)* — رحلة
riHla

trousers — بنطلون
banTaloon

true — صح
SaHH

trunk *(US: car)* — شنطة السيارة
shanTat
as-sayyaara

try — جرب
jarrab,
yejarrib — يجرب

T-shirt — تي شيرت
'tee-shirt'

Tuesday — يوم الثلاثاء
yowm
ath-thulathaa

Tunisia — تونس
toones (f)

tunnel — نفق
nafaq

tweezers — ملقاط
milqaaT

tyre — إطار
'iTaar

U

ugly — قبيح
qabeeH

umbrella — شمسية
shamsiya

uncle — خال
khaal

under *(prep)* — تحت
taHt

underpants — كلسون
kalsoon

understand — فهم
fahem,
yafham — يفهم

**United Arab
Emirates** — الإمارات
al-'imaaraat (f)

United States — امريكا
amreeka

university — جامعة
jaamiAa

unpleasant — مو طيب
moo Tayyib

until — حتى
Hattaa

up: up there — فوق
fowq

upstairs — فوق
fowq

urgent — عاجل
Aajil

us — احنا
iHna;
(see grammar)

use *(verb)* — استعمل
'istaAmal,
yastaAmil — يسترمل

useful — مفيد
mufeed

usually — عادة
Aadatan

V

vaccination — تلقيح
talqeeH

valid — ساري
saaree
al-mafʻool — المفعول

115

ENGLISH-ARABIC

W

English	Arabic
valley waadee	وادي
van shaaHena	شاحنة
vanilla al-faneela	الفنيلا
vase vaaza	فازة
VD maraD tanaasulee	مرض تناسلي
veal laHm Aajal	لحم عجل
vegetables khuDar	خضر
vegetarian nabatee	نباتي
very jiddan	جداً
very good kwayis jiddan	كويس جداً
very hot Haarr jiddan	حار جداً
very much katheer jiddan	كثير جداً
video shareeT al-veediyoo	شريط الفيديو
village qariya	قرية
vinegar khall	خل
visa ta'sheerat safar	تأشيرة سفر
visit (verb) zaar, yazoor	زار يزور
voice Sowt	صوت

English	Arabic
waist khaSr	خصر
wait 'intaZar, yantaZir	انتظر ينتظر
waiter garsoon	جرسون
wake up (oneself) SaHa, yaSHa	صحى يصحى
walk (verb) meshi, yamshee	مشى يمشي
walkman(R) 'walkman'	والكمن
wall Haa'iT	حائط
wallet miHfaZa	محفظة
want araad, yureed	اراد يريد
I want ureed	أريد
do you want ...? tureed ...?	تريد ... ؟
war Harb	حرب
warm: it's warm daafi'	دافئ
wash (something) ghasal, yaghsil	غسل يغسل
(oneself) 'istaHamm, yastaHimm	استحم يستحم

116

ENGLISH-ARABIC

washbasin	حوض الغسل	weekend	نهاية الاسبوع
HowD al-ghasl		nihaayat	
washing powder	مسحوق	al-osbooA	
masHooq	الغسيل	weight	وزن
al-ghaseel		wazn	
wasp	زنبور	welcome: you're	
zanboor		welcome	عفوا
watch (for time)	ساعة	Aafwan	
saAa		welcome!	مرحبا !
watch (verb)		marHaban!	
tafarraj,	تفرج	well (health)	جيد
yatfarraj	يتفرج	jayyid	
water	مية	he's well	صحته جيدة
moya		SiHHatu jayyida	
water melon	بطيخ	he's not well	هو مريض
baTTeekh		huwwa mareeD	
way: this way		well (adverb)	طيب
(like this)	كذا	Tayyib	
kiza		west	غرب
can you tell me		gharb	
the way to		wet	مبلل
the ...?		muballal	
mumkin	ممكن تقول	what?	ايش ؟
taqool lee	لي واين ... ؟	eesh?	
wayn ...?		what's this?	ايش هذا ؟
we	احنا	eesh haaza?	
iHna;		wheel	عجلة
(see grammar)		Aajala	
weak	ضعيف	when?	متى ؟
DaAeef		mita?	
weather	طقس	where?	اين ؟
Taqs		ayn?	
wedding	زفاف	which: which	
zafaaf		one?	اي واحد ؟
Wednesday	يوم الأربعاء	ayy waaHid?	
yowm		white	ابيض
al-arbiAaa'		abyaD	
week	أسبوع	who?	من ؟
osbooA		man?	

ENGLISH-ARABIC

whose?	لمن ؟	word	كلمة
limeen?		kilma	
whose is this?	لمن هذا ؟	**work** (noun)	شغل
limeen haaza?		shoghl	
why?	ليه ؟	work (verb)	
leeh?		'ishtaghal,	اشتغل
wide	واسع	yashtaghil	يشتغل
waasiA		it's not working	مو شغال
wife	زوجة	moo shaghaal	
zowja		world	العالم
win		al-Aalam	
faaz,	فاز	worse	اسوء
yafooz	يفوز	aswa'	
wind	ريح	wrench	مفتاح براغي
reeH (f)		miftaaH	
window	شباك	beraaghee	
shubbaak		wrist	معصم
windscreen	الزجاج	miASam	
az-zujaaj	الامامي	write	
al-amaamee		katab,	كتب
wine	خمر	yaktub	يكتب
khamr		wrong	خطأ
winter	فصل الشتاء	khaTa'	
faSl ash-shitaa'			
wire	سلك		
seelk		**Y**	
with	مع		
maAa			
without	بدون	year	سنة
bidoon		sana	
without ice	بدون ثلج	yellow	اسفر
bidoon thalj		aSfar	
woman	حرمة	Yemen	اليمن
Horma		al-yaman (f)	
wonderful	رائع	yes	نعم
raa'iA		naAam	
wood	خشب	oh yes I do!	اكيد !
khashab		akeed!	
wool	صوف	yesterday	أمس
Soof		ams	

118

ENGLISH-ARABIC

the day before		**zoo**	حديقة
yesterday	أول أمس	Hadeeqat	الحيوانات
awwal ams		al-Hayawaanaat	
yet: not yet	لسة		
lissa			
yoghurt	لبن زبادي		
laban zabaadee			
you (to a man)			
anta	انت		
(to a woman)			
anti	انت		
(plural)			
antum;	انتم		
(see grammar)			
young	شاب		
shaab			
young people	شبان		
shubbaan			
your (singular)			
...-ek	...ك		
your book			
kitaabek	كتابك		
(plural)			
...-kum	...كم		
your book			
kitaabkum;	كتابكم		
(see grammar)			
yours (singular)			
milkek	ملكك		
(plural)			
milk-kum	ملككم		

zero	صفر
Sifr	
zip	سوستة
soosta	

GRAMMAR

The *DEFINITE ARTICLE*, **the**, is indicated by the particle 'al-' added to the beginning of the noun. Although it is always written the same in Arabic script, it is pronounced differently depending on the initial consonant of the word that follows. If the word begins with t, T, d, D, s, S, z, Z, n or r, the '-l-' in 'al-' is not pronounced and the next consonant is doubled:

al-kitaab **the book**   ad-darraaja **the bicycle**
ar-rajul **the man**

There is no equivalent of the *INDEFINITE ARTICLE*, **a** or **an**, in Arabic. For example:

rajul can mean **man** or **a man**.

NOUNS in Arabic are either masculine or feminine. Nouns ending in a consonant are usually masculine:

Tabeeb **doctor**   kitaab **book**   dars **lesson**

With a few exceptions (shown in the English-Arabic dictionary), feminine nouns can be recognised by the '-a' ending:

sayyaara **car**   Haqeeba **bag**

Many feminine nouns are formed by adding '-a' to masculine nouns:

Tabeeb **doctor** *(m)*   Tabeeba **doctor** *(f)*
Aamm **uncle**   Aamma **aunt**

To make a regular *MASCULINE PLURAL* you simply add '-oon' to the singular:

muAallim **teacher**   muHaasib **accountant**
muAallimoon **teachers** muHaasiboon **accountants**

To make a regular *FEMININE PLURAL*, you remove the '-a' ending and substitute '-aat'. So for example:

sayaara **car**   tuffaaHa **apple**
sayaaraat **cars**   tuffaaHaat **apples**

Unlike English, *ADJECTIVES* in Arabic are placed after

GRAMMAR

the noun they describe. They must agree with that noun in number and gender. The form given in the dictionary of this book is the masculine singular. The feminine form is obtained by adding '-a' to the end of the adjective. If the noun is definite the adjective is definite too, and 'al-' (or its appropriate form) is repeated before the adjective:

kitaab	**a book**
kitaab jadeed	**a new book**
al-kitaab al-jadeed	**the new book**
sayaara	**a car**
sayaara Sagheera	**a small car**
al-sayaara aS-Sagheera	**the small car**
rajul	**a man**
rajul Tayyib	**a nice man**
al-rajul aT-Tayyib	**the nice man**

Masculine plural adjectives describing humans are formed by adding the ending '**-aa**' or '**-aar**':

tulaab shuTaar	**clever students**
saa'iHoon ingleeziyaa	**English tourists**
aTfaal sughraa	**small children**

Feminine plural adjectives describing humans are formed by adding the ending '**-aat**':

Hormaat shaabaat	**young women**
sayidaat ingleeziyaat	**English ladies**

However, non-human plural nouns take the feminine singular of the adjective, regardless of whether they are masculine or feminine:

shunuT thaqeela	**heavy suitcases** *(m)*
fanaadiq rakheesa	**cheap hotels** *(m)*
shaqqaat kabeera	**large flats** *(f)*
Halwaat kwayisa	**nice sweets** *(f)*

To form the *COMPARATIVE* of most adjectives an 'a-' is added at the beginning and the vowels in the word are changed to 'a':

adjective	*comparative*
baAeed **far**	abAad **farther**
ghaali **expensive**	aghla **more expensive**
kabeer **big**	akbar **bigger**

GRAMMAR

rakheeS **cheap**	arkhaS **cheaper**
Sagheer **small**	aSghar **smaller**
sahl **easy**	as-hal **easier**
Taweel **long, tall**	aTwal **longer, taller**
kwayiss **good**	aHsan **better** *(irregular)*

al-qaahira akbar min Aammaan   huwwa aTwal minee
Cairo is bigger than Amman   **he is taller than me**

To form the *SUPERLATIVE* an 'al-' is added to the comparative, for example:

al-abAad **farthest**	al-aSghar **smallest**
al-aghla **most expensive**	al-as-hal **easiest**
al-akbar **biggest**	al-aTwal **longest, tallest**
al-arkhaS **cheapest**	al-aHsan **best**

The usual way of forming *ADVERBS* is to add the ending '-an', (or '-yan' if the adjective ends in a vowel) to the adjective:

baTee' **slow**	baTee'an **slowly**
Halee **current**	Haaliyan **currently**

There are no *POSSESSIVE ADJECTIVES* as such in Arabic; instead a suffix is added to the noun:

noun ending in vowel	noun ending in consonant	
-tee	-ee	**my**
-tek*	-ek*	**your** *(sing)*
-tu	-u	**his**
-t-ha	-ha	**her**
-t-na	-na	**our**
-t-kum	-kum	**your** *(pl)*
-t-hum	-hum	**their**

*'-tek' (or '-ek') is usually heard for both masculine and feminine and the gender is usually clear from the context

sayaara **car**	baytu **his house**
sayaarat-ha **her car**	baladna **our country**

POSSESSIVE PRONOUNS are as follows:

milkee **mine**	milknaa **ours**
milkek **yours** *(sing)*	milkum **yours** *(pl)*
milku **his**	milkhum **theirs**
milkaa **hers**	

122

GRAMMAR

al-qameeS milku **the shirt is his**
al-bayt milkhum **the house is theirs**

PERSONAL PRONOUNS are as follows:

ana **I**	iHna **we**
anta **you** *(to a man)*	antum **you** *(pl)*
anti **you** *(to a woman)*	
huwwa **he**	hum **they**
hiyya **she**	

Personal pronouns can be omitted when the form of the verb makes it obvious who the subject is:

(ana) kuntu taAbaan **I was tired**
kaanat jameela **she was beautiful**

DIRECT and *INDIRECT OBJECT PRONOUNS* take the form of a suffix added onto the end of the verb and are as follows:

direct object

-nee **me**	-na **us**
-ak **you** *(to a man)*	-kum **you** *(pl)*
-ik **you** *(to a woman)*	
-u **him, it**	-hum **them** *(people)*
-ha **her, it, them** *(things)*	

Darabnee	**he hit me**
ishtaraytuha	**I bought them**
aHibbak	**I love you** *(to a man)*
aHibbik	**I love you** *(to a woman)*

indirect object

-lee **to me**	-lena **to us**
-lak **to you** *(to a man)*	-lekum **to you** *(pl)*
-lik **to you** *(to a woman)*	
-lu **to him, to it**	-lehum **to them**
-leha **to her, to it**	

arsalatlena khiTaab	**she sent (to) us a letter**
qullee!	**tell me!**
waAdnalekum An ...	**we promised (to) you that ...**

REFLEXIVE PRONOUNS all begin with the word 'nafs' meaning 'self' and are as follows:

nafsee **myself**   nafsna **ourselves**

123

GRAMMAR

nafsak **yourself** (*to a man*) nafskum **yourselves**
nafsik **yourself** (*to a woman*)
nafsu **himself** nafshun **themselves**
nafsaha **herself**

In Arabic, there is no present tense of the verb *TO BE*
'kaan/yakoon':

al-ghurfa ghaaliya **the room is expensive**
(*the room expensive*)

at-taksee hina **the taxi is here** (*the taxi here*)

hiyya taAbaana **she is tired** (*she tired*)

In the past tense, the following forms are used:

kuntu **I was** kuna **we were**
kunta **you were** (*to a man*) kuntum **you were** (*pl*)
kunti **you were** (*to a woman*)
kaan **he was, it was** (*m*) kaanoo **they were** (*people*)
kaanat **she was, it was** (*f*),
    they were (*things*)

(ana) kuntu AaTshaan **I was thirsty**
kaanat naa'ima **she was asleep**
kaan mareeD **he was ill**

In the future tense the following forms are used:

sa-akoon **I shall be**
sa-takoon **you will be** (*to a man*)
sa-takoonee **you will be** (*to a woman*)
sa-yakoon **he will be, it will be** (*m*)
sa-tatkoon **she will be, it will be** (*f*),
    they will be (*things*)
sa-nakoon **we shall be**
sa-takoonoo **you will be** (*pl*)
sa-yakoonoo **they will be** (*people*)

sa-nakoon met'akhareen **we shall be late**
sa-akoon hina **I shall be here**

The present tense of *TO HAVE* is formed as follows:

Andee **I have** Andana **we have**
Andak **you have** (*to a man*) Andukum **you have** (*pl*)
Andik **you have** (*to a woman*)
Anduh **he has, it has** (*m*) Anduhum **they have**
    (*people*)
And-ha **she has, it has** (*f*),
    they have (*things*)

124

GRAMMAR

The infinitive *VERB* form does not exist in Arabic. Under each verb in the dictionary we have given two forms. The first form is the masculine singular perfect from which you can form any part of the past tense. The second form is the masculine singular imperfect from which you can form any part of the present or future tense.

In cases where English uses the *PRESENT TENSE* of a verb, Arabic uses the second of the two verb forms given in the dictionary:

yaktub	**write**
aktub	**I write, I am writing etc** (omit the 'y')
taktub	**you write** *(to a man)* (replace the 'y' with 't')
taktubee	**you write** *(to a woman)* (replace the 'y' with a 't' and add '-ee')
yaktub	**he writes**
taktub	**she writes** (replace 'y' with 't')
naktub	**we write** (replace 'y' with 'n')
taktuboo	**you write** (replace 'y' with 't' and add '-oo')
yaktuboo	**they write** (add '-oo')

ana antaZir Sadeeqee   **I am waiting for my friend**

The *PAST TENSE* of a verb is formed by taking the first form of the verb given in the dictionary and adding the appropriate endings (note that the stress moves):

katab	**write**
katabtu	**I wrote** (add -tu)
katabta	**you wrote** *(to a man)* (add -ta)
katabti	**you wrote** *(to a woman)* (add -tee)
katab	**he wrote**
katabat	**she wrote** (add -at)
katabna	**we wrote** (add -na)
katabtum	**you wrote** *(pl)* (add -tum)
kataboo	**they wrote** (add -oo)

The *FUTURE* tense is produced by adding the prefix 'sa-' to the present tense:

yaktub	**write**
sa-aktub	**I shall write** (omit the 'y')
sa-taktub	**you will write** *(to a man)* (replace the 'y' with 't')
sa-taktubee	**you will write** *(to a woman)* (replace the 'y' with a 't' and add '-ee')
sa-yaktub	**he will write**

GRAMMAR

sa-taktub	**she will write** (replace 'y' with 't')
sa-naktub	**we shall write** (replace 'y' with 'n')
sa-taktuboo	**you will write** (replace 'y' with 't' and add '-oo')
sa-yaktuboo	**they will write** (add '-oo')

This model can be used for all forms given in this book apart from 'to be', see p 124 above.

raaH/yerooH **go**
bukra sa-arooH ila al-qahira **tomorrow I'll go to Cairo**

arsal/yersil **send**
sa-nersil ilaykum khiTaab fish-shahr al-qaadim
we shall send you a letter next month

There are two sorts of *IMPERATIVE* - the positive as in **go!**, **stand up!** and the negative as in **don't go!**, **don't come!** etc.

To form the positive imperative you take the second form of the verb given in this book. For example, from **stop** you take 'yatawaqaf' and make the following changes:

If speaking to a man, omit the 'ya':

tawaqaf! **stop!**

If speaking to a woman, omit the 'ya' and add '-ee':

tawaqafee! **stop!**

If speaking to several people, omit the 'ya' and add '-oo':

tawaqafoo! **stop!**

To form a negative imperative - take the future **you** form of the verb (in this case 'tatawaqaf' - **you will stop**) and put 'laa' **do not** before it:

laa tatawaqaf! **don't stop!**

The Arabic words for *IT* in many cases is 'huwwa', which also means **he**. 'It' can sometimes be translated by 'hiyya', which also means **she**:

huwwa haarr **it's hot**   huwwa milkaa **it's hers**

In Arabic the way of forming the *NEGATIVE* varies according to whether the verb is in the past, future or present tense.

In the present tense you put the word 'mu' before the verb you want to negate:

ana aktub khiTaab **I am writing a letter**
ana mu aktub khiTaab **I am not writing a letter**

In the past tense you put the word 'maa' before the verb:

ana riHtu ilal-sooq haza aS-SabaaH
I went to the market this morning

ana maa riHtu ilal-sooq haza aS-SabaaH
I didn't go to the market this morning

In the future tense you have a choice of negatives. To make a general negative place 'maa' before the verb:

sa-yakoon feel-maTAm haza al-masaa
he will be at the restaurant tonight

maa sa-yakoon feel-maTAm haza al-masaa
he won't be at the restaurant tonight

To make the negative more emphatic you can use 'lan' instead of 'maa'. The implication with 'lan' is **never** or **extremely unlikely** or **no way**.

There are eleven common *PREPOSITIONS* in Arabic:

Ala	**on** *(upon)*	fowq	**above, on top of**
And	**equivalent to**	li	**to, for**
	French **chez**	maAa	**with**
baAd	**after**	min	**from**
bi	**at, in**	qabl	**before**
fee	**in**	taHt	**under**

The preposition always comes immediately before the word it relates to. If the preposition ends in a vowel and is followed by 'al-' (**the**), it is merged with the 'al-':

huwa fee ghurfatih **he's in his room**
al-finjaan AlaT-Taawila **the cup is on the table**
al-shanta taHt as-sareer **the suitcase is under the bed**

Arabic makes a *QUESTION* from a statement very simply. You put the word 'hal' at the beginning of the statement, leaving the word order the same. You also change the intonation of the sentence, the voice usually rising noticeably at the end:

aHmed hina **Ahmed is here**
hal aHmed hina? **is Ahmed here?**

In very colloquial usage you do not even have to put 'hal' at the beginning - you just put the statement in a querying tone of voice:

aHmed hina? **is Ahmed here?**

CONVERSION TABLES

metres

1 metre = 39.37 inches or 1.09 yards

kilometres

1 kilometre = 0.62 or approximately $^5/_8$ mile

to convert kilometres to miles: divide by 8 and multiply by 5

kilometres:	2	3	4	5	10	100
miles:	1.25	1.90	2.5	3.1	6.25	62.5

miles

to convert miles to kilometres: divide by 5 and multiply by 8

miles:	1	3	5	10	20	100
kilometres:	1.6	4.8	8	16	32	160

kilos

1 kilo = 2.2 or approximately $^{11}/_5$ pounds

to convert kilos to pounds: divide by 5 and multiply by 11

kilos:	4	5	10	20	30	40
pounds:	8.8	11	22	44	66	88

pounds

1 pound = 0.45 or approximately $^5/_{11}$ kilo

litres

1 litre = approximately $^{13}/_4$ pints or 0.22 gallons

Celsius

to convert to Fahrenheit: divide by 5, multiply by 9, add 32

Celsius:	10	15	20	25	28	30	34
Fahrenheit:	50	59	68	77	82	86	93

Fahrenheit

to convert Fahrenheit to Celsius: subtract 32, multiply by 5, divide by 9